HOW TO
WATERSAFE
INFANTS & TODDLERS

Lana E. Whitehead & Lindsay R. Curtis, M.D.
Illustrated by Paul Farber

HPBooks

Authors Lindsay Curtis and Lana Whitehead.

HPBooks

Publishers: Bill and Helen Fisher
Executive Editor: Rick Bailey
Editorial Director: Randy Summerlin
Editor: Judith Schuler
Art Director: Don Burton
Book Design: Leslie Sinclair
Illustrations: Paul Farber
Photography: Tim Fuller
Cover photograph: Gill Kenny

ACKNOWLEDGMENTS

We wish to thank Mary Reeve for her help in producing this book, Gordon Whitehead for the photographs that enabled the artist to illustrate the techniques of our methods, and Ida S. Brown for her devotion to us and our project.

Many physicians have contributed time and counsel as we attempted to portray the hazards and virtues of teaching children. We appreciate their help.

ABOUT THE AUTHORS

Lana E. Whitehead is one of the most well-known swimming instructors in the United States. She has a B.A. in Physical Education and has been teaching swimming for over 12 years. Her goal has been to teach young children to swim. Her methods are unique because she deals with very young children—those ranging in age from 3 months to 4 years. She has instructed over 10,000 infants and toddlers in her program. Lana and her unique methods have been featured on national television programs such as **That's Incredible, PM Magazine** and **The Body Human.**

Lindsay R. Curtis, M.D., is a retired physician from Ogden, Utah. He obtained his B.A. degree from the University of Utah and his M.D. from the University of Colorado School of Medicine. He is a Fellow of the American College of Obstetrics and Gynecology, a Diplomate of the American Board of Obstetrics and Gynecology and was an Assistant Clinical Professor of Obstetrics and Gynecology at the University of Utah College of Medicine. He was also educational counsultant for the Utah Division of the American Cancer Society.

Dr. Curtis is also the author of the best-selling **Pregnant & Lovin' It** and **How To Save A Life Using CPR,** both published by HPBooks.

HPBooks
P.O. Box 5367
Tucson, AZ 85703 (602) 888-2150
ISBN: 0-89586-215-8
Library of Congress Catalog Card Number: 82-84459
© 1983 Fisher Publishing, Inc.
Printed in U.S.A.

Cover Photograph: Learning water safety and survival techniques is fun, as this mother and child demonstrate at Canyon Ranch Resort in Tucson, Arizona.

Getting Ready 5

Your Child's Development 23

Infant Program 45

Toddler Program 65

Questions & Answers 91

Index 96

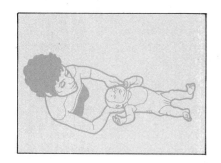

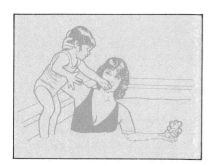

Getting Ready

This book will teach you how to make your child watersafe. By the time you finish this step-by-step course, you and your youngster will have successfully learned an important life-saving skill together.

It takes patience and love, but it's *fun,* too! The hours you spend in the pool with your child may be some of the most delightful moments of his childhood.

What Is Watersafe?

Aaron was only 2 years old, but not too young to climb a fence and fall in the family swimming pool. When his mother noticed he was missing, she rushed to the pool in panic. There she found her toddler confidently floating on his back.

In a freak boating accident, 1-year-old Tara was thrown from a boat and landed under the dock. The boat lodged against the dock so the little girl couldn't be rescued until the dock was torn apart. In spite of this delay, when rescuers finally reached her, they found Tara safely floating on her back.

These and other accidents could have resulted in fatal tragedies if their young victims had not been trained in water safety and survival. When

A watersafe toddler can confidently float on his back.

we say a youngster is *watersafe,* we mean he can save his life if he accidently falls in the water.

How can an infant or toddler save his own life? Watch a child who has completed this training. When he is placed in a body of water, he immediately goes underwater, then turns over on his back to float. A child who has completed the course can float on his back independently, relaxed and breathing easily.

But this *survival float* is not all a watersafe child can do. He can also propel himself in the direction of the wall of the pool, grasp the edge and keep his head out of the water!

Babies 3 to 9 months old *kick-glide* through the water on their stomachs, then turn on their backs to take a breath. Children 14 months and older learn to lift their heads to take regular breaths while they *kick-paddle* through the water.

Using our method, you can teach your child to do these things in the swimming pool. You can chart his progress on the achievement scorecards on pages 63 and 89. When finished, you will have the peace of mind that comes from knowing he is watersafe.

WATERSAFE IS *NOT* DROWNPROOF

When your child has completed this course, he will respect the water, feel comfortable and know how to survive in it. But he is still *not drownproof.* No child is *ever* drownproof. Even after completing this training, never leave an infant or toddler unattended in or near water.

A pool may have a wall around it, but there may be a gate your child can open. An irrigation ditch, river, creek or pond might be uninteresting to you, but it can be a dangerous attraction to a curious toddler. Never leave your child alone when he is around *any* kind of water.

Your child may be watersafe, but it doesn't mean he knows how to *swim.* He can propel himself to the wall by kicking and using a paddle-type arm stroke, but advanced swimming skills come later.

Your child may be swimming like a fish at the age of 2. He may learn his advanced skills from group swimming classes or from individualized lessons taught by you. But before he learns to swim, your child should become *watersafe.* This is the life-saving purpose of this book.

STATISTICS

Each year about 6,000 accidental drownings occur in the United States. More than 12% of these accidents happen in swimming pools. These

Never leave your infant or toddler when he's in or around water.

figures are higher in the warmer states, where backyard pools are common.

Many drowning victims are infants and toddlers. In Arizona, for example, 27% of the drownings in 1982 involved children in the under-5 age group. As a cause of death to young children, drowning is second only to traffic accidents.

Most drownings are preventable. Even though infants and toddlers are too young to benefit from most formal group swimming lessons, they *can* learn to be safe in the water. All they need is patient, individualized instruction.

Our Method

For more than 12 years, our method has been used to teach thousands of infants and toddlers water safety and survival. Out of this experience has come the program you will learn in this book.

The method is built on sound physiological and educational principles. It uses a detailed system of patterning and behavior modification. Gradually you will modify your child's basic instinctive responses and turn them into life-saving water-safety techniques.

As the teacher, you modify behavior and teach life-saving techniques.

The three most important ingredients of this program are *success, love* and *play*. You will combine all three as you communicate with your child in the water.

SUCCESS BREEDS SUCCESS

This method is built around success. We've never had a child who failed to learn the skills. Some take longer than others, but every child succeeds within his own capacity—even the handicapped.

Positive reinforcement by the parent is the secret of this success. Your child quickly responds to your positive attitude and recognition of his accomplishments. As you praise him, a close tie develops between you and your child.

This program of positive reinforcement helps build your child's self-confidence. Confidence in himself is important to his future performance in life. You're teaching him success as a habit.

LOVE AND TRUST

This method builds a parent-child relationship. Your hugging, soothing, comforting and singing help your child overcome his fear and resistance.

You become your child's best friend.

There is no screaming, crying or looks of fear when you're with your child in the pool. Instead there are hugs, kisses and laughter as you develop a bond of love and trust together.

This special bond is one of the greatest parts of this training. Because your child trusts you completely, you become closer to each other.

PLAY IS IMPORTANT

Play is a major ingredient of this program. A firm rule is intersperse play with work.

Work is interspersed throughout a lesson. Work is not done all at once. The fun you have with your child in the water provides his motivation to learn. So be sure to play *and* work.

Actually, the word *work* is not appropriate for the kind of teaching you do. Each activity is filled with songs and happy games. Your child has a delightful time laughing and learning. He may not even realize he is being taught.

Communication Grows—As you develop the patience necessary for this teaching process, you learn about communicating with your child. You will be amazed at how much you discover about him—his needs and his capabilities. Both of you will look back on this time as enjoyable.

Your expressions of love, confidence and approval of your child and his efforts are essential to this program. Recognition of accomplishment and praise for effort can become desirable habits for you. They also become important confidence-builders for your child.

Love Is Stronger—You will be in frequent physical contact with your infant or toddler as you hug and support him in the water. This physical contact is comforting and strengthens the bond of love between you.

Everyone has a basic need to love and be loved, to appreciate and be appreciated. We have the desire to need and be needed, to achieve and be recognized for achievement. This training provides opportunities to meet all of these needs and more. It helps strengthen the bond of love between you and your child.

YOUR CHILD AS AN INDIVIDUAL

We will discuss the actions and reactions you can expect from the *average* child. But *no* child is average. Each child has a unique personality, and each develops at his own pace.

If your infant or toddler doesn't show the same responses as those mentioned on these pages, don't be discouraged. Time schedules are only general guidelines.

Your child may need more or less time to learn a specific skill. He may require several days or even weeks before he begins to feel comfortable in the water.

Be patient and loving. You know your own child's needs and feelings better than anyone else. Take your time, and you will learn and have fun together.

Sex and Age—For simplicity, in this book we use the masculine pronoun *he* to refer to all infants and toddlers. This doesn't reflect a preference for boys. We expect parents of daughters will mentally substitute the pronoun *she*.

We've tried to keep things simple by using different terms for different age groups. By *infants* we mean all children under 9 months old. The general term *toddlers* means youngsters from 9 months to 4 years old. *Younger toddlers* are 9 months to 15 months, and *older toddlers* are 15 months to 4 years.

In presenting lessons, we have considered both younger and older toddlers in the same section of this book. We do this because the same teaching techniques are effective for both age groups. Three-year-olds may learn their skills faster than younger toddlers, but they learn them in the same manner.

Your time in the pool strengthens the love between you and your child.

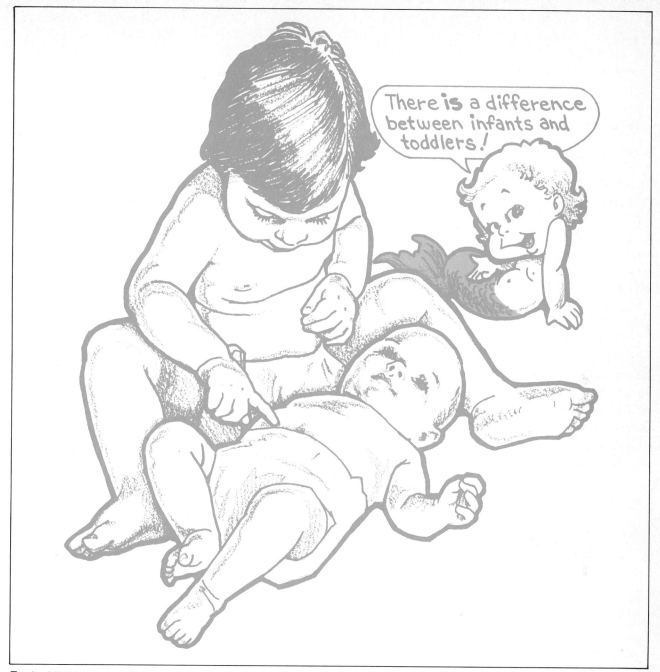

Each child develops at his own pace so don't compare your child to other children.

Your Role as a Parent

Many parents prefer to drop their child at a swimming class twice a week. After a few months, have the satisfaction of knowing he has learned to swim. But what about infants and toddlers who are too young to be accepted in many swimming groups? Unfortunately, youngsters under 4 years old are the most drown-prone.

Special classes by qualified instructors are increasing for younger age groups, but the majority of parents still have to teach their children to be watersafe. Having used the method presented in this book with thousands of infants and toddlers, we *know* it works. If you as parents accept the assignment, this book will help you accomplish the task.

Enthusiasm and Determination—Because this program is a one-to-one type of training, your enthusiasm as a teacher is essential to your success. Your child senses your sincere enthusiasm and responds with eager interest.

Determination and strict adherence to the instructions are important, too. Like a well-planned reducing diet, this program is only as effective as

Mothers often give lessons, but fathers make excellent teachers, too.

the individual carrying it out. The rules of the method are rigid, but success is assured when they are faithfully followed.

MOM OR DAD?

Ideally, both parents become involved in teaching their child water safety and survival. They take turns giving him lessons on a one-to-one basis.

Other people may not agree with your decision to begin water-safety training.

More often, though, one parent takes the initiative or has the talent for teaching. Often this is the mother. For this reason, the instructions in the book are mainly directed to mothers.

Fathers make excellent teachers, too. We hope fathers will participate whenever possible. Love and trust are the most important teaching tools in this program. Either parent can use them with equal effectiveness.

KEEP IT ONE-TO-ONE

When you are teaching your child in the pool, give him your full attention. If you do, he'll be more likely to give you his. It's better not to have another adult or child in the pool with you during the lesson. Even if the other person is his father, your youngster's attention will be distracted from what you are trying to teach him.

The same applies for an older brother or sister who already knows how to swim. An older sibling should not be playing in the pool while you are teaching. Instead, he should watch the lesson and pay attention to what you are doing. When he understands what your infant or toddler must learn, he can become an enthusiastic teacher. He can later join you in the water and work with his younger brother or sister himself. Children learn well from each other.

IGNORE DISCOURAGEMENT

Many people may try to discourage you in your efforts. They tell you your infant or toddler is

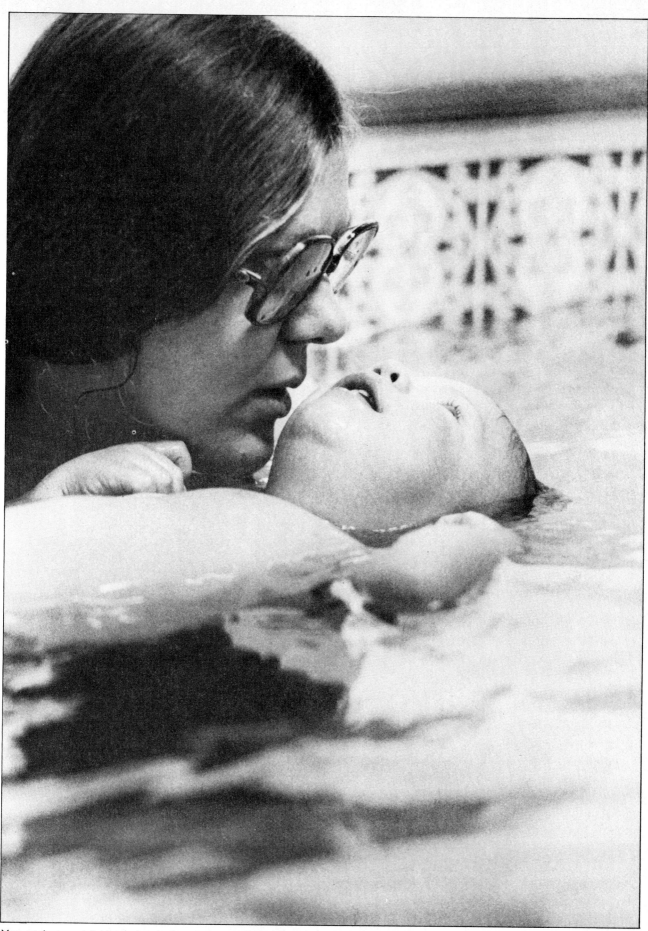

You and your child learn best when you can devote full attention to each other.

Your baby lived in water in the uterus for nine months.

"too young to learn" or he will be "frightened and frustrated." They say you're unqualified or the water causes upper-respiratory infections.

All these allegations are false. Ignore them and persist with your efforts. It's your child's life you're protecting.

He Will Be Healthy—Pediatricians who care for children taking water-safety training often find these children have fewer colds and infections. This could be due to the good physical conditioning that comes from regular exercise in the water. In any case, there is no indication youngsters who spend time in swimming pools have more infections than those who do not.

He Will Learn—One philosopher stated that man is not just a human being—he is a *human becoming*. So is your child. Research confirms that constant stimulation to a baby's brain facilitates early physical, intellectual and social development.

The special relationship that develops between you and your child gives you the opportunity to bring out the best in him. Basic reflexes can be trained to become responses that can save his life in these early years.

Bonus of Confidence—As an added bonus, the self-confidence your child gains through these lessons will help him when he tackles other learning challenges. He will have discovered how to achieve through determination and hard work. He will become a self-motivated individual who is responsible for his own actions.

So don't listen to discouraging words. The loving trust your child has in you makes you the best person to teach him to be watersafe!

WHEN TO START

A newborn baby has just completed 9 months of living in water in his mother's uterus. A person might think he is able to begin water-safety and survival training as soon as he is born.

This is true. We have successfully trained many newborns. However, teaching newborn babies requires skill few instructors possess.

In general, 3 months old is a good time to begin water-safety and survival training for your child. By baby's third month, you will have sufficiently regained your strength to undertake the program.

If your child is older than 3 months, the time to begin is *now!* The sooner you begin, the sooner he will be watersafe.

Where And When

The ideal teaching environment is a private, heated swimming pool in a quiet neighborhood.

WATER TEMPERATURE
The water should be about the same temperature as your child's bath water—88F (31C) in the summer and up to 92F (33C) in cooler weather.

If you can't find a heated pool, wait until the hottest months of summer. Teach your child only on warm, sunny days. If recent rain has chilled the pool, postpone the lesson.

Infants hate and fear cold water. They may remember their days in the uterus, when they lived in water that was 98.6F (37C). *Never force your child to go into a pool that's too chilly!* You can't teach him anything when he's crying and covered with goosebumps.

TYPES OF POOLS
You have several options in choosing a swimming pool.

Outdoor Pools—These should be heated or naturally warmed from the summer sun. You can't use them in bad weather, but they have advantages. It's pleasant being outdoors with your child in the sunshine.

Indoor Pools—A warm indoor pool allows you to schedule your lessons in any kind of weather. It also solves the problem of sunburn. It's probably quieter than an outdoor pool. Private indoor pools are hard to find, however. Privacy is important to the success of these lessons.

Public Pools—Because of the importance of privacy, public pools are a last resort. Some do not accept infants because of public health rules and insurance considerations. Those that admit babies have the disadvantage of noisy crowds. It's almost impossible to teach a child who is constantly being distracted.

If you don't have your own pool, try to find a friend or neighbor who does. Perhaps you can find a pool owner who is also the parent of an infant or toddler. The two of you can begin the water-safety training together, but always give your lessons separately.

ALTERNATIVES TO SWIMMING POOLS
If you can't find a private pool, there are other places to teach your child water safety.

Spas—Spas are becoming more popular. If you or a friend don't own one, you may find a place that rents them by the hour.

Make sure that the water is not warmer than 95F (35C). Higher temperatures are not healthy for young children.

Never turn on the bubbling air jets. They are distracting and can be dangerous for your child.

Lakes, Oceans—In the summer months, a warm, clean lake can be used for teaching water safety. Choose days when the water is calm—high waves can frighten your child.

The ocean is fun for a child after he learns to swim. During the time he is learning water safety, it can seem frightening. Saltwater can hurt his eyes. If he drinks it, he won't like the taste. Even if the water is warm, it isn't wise to try to teach your child water safety in the ocean.

Bathtubs, Plastic Wading Pools—Use these to teach your child to enjoy the water. Make bath time a happy time of day, filled with games and songs. When your child is in a wading pool, let him play with his toys in the water.

Water should be slightly cooler than the 98.6F (37C) temperature of the uterus.

High waves, cold temperatures and saltwater can frighten your child.

Play makes learning water safety more fun.

You can teach some basic water-safety skills in the tub or wading pool. Your child can learn to put his face in the water, blow bubbles and breathe out. He can practice kicking and paddling.

Try demonstrating water-safety skills with your child's favorite doll. He will love to imitate its actions.

HOW LONG? HOW OFTEN?

The recommended time for lessons is 30 minutes. Devote enough time to play to keep your child interested in the lessons. Try to schedule time in the pool every day to keep your child from forgetting what he learns each lesson.

Daily lessons also have the advantage of keeping you going from force of habit. Even if your child seems to be stuck on a progress plateau, continue to go to the pool and teach him every day. We realize that busy mothers can't always get to a pool every day. If you can't, schedule your child's lessons as frequently as possible.

Keep your lessons *regular*. Always teach on Monday, Wednesday and Friday or some other repeated pattern of days. Let force of habit help you persist in your goal.

Lesson Breaks—If illness or some other event forces a break in the lessons, don't expect your child to pick up and go on from where you left off. Start over again. Don't be impatient. Your child soon relearns forgotten skills and goes on to become watersafe.

TIME OF DAY

Schedule your lessons when the pool is quiet and you can be alone. If you use a friend's or neighbor's pool, choose a time when he or she is not at home.

Daily Routine—Think about your child's normal daily routine and schedule your lesson around it. You want to teach your child during the happiest time of his day.

Wait at least an hour after he's had a meal. Food and swallowed water may cause vomiting. Be sure your child isn't hungry for his next feeding or meal. He will think only of food, not about what you are teaching.

Make sure your child is not tired. Many mothers teach their children right after their naps.

Position of the Sun—The glare of the sun on the water can be irritating and distracting. It's difficult to teach a child to float on his back if he must look directly at the sun.

After his nap, he's happy and attentive.

In the summer, your child can get sunburned. Even if you use sunscreen, it may wash off in the water.

For these reasons, choose a time of day when the sun is behind a house, tree or other barrier. Or schedule your lesson at a time when the sun is at an angle. Midmorning or late afternoon are good times for teaching.

Storms—Unless you use an indoor pool, *never give a lesson during a storm!* When your child complains about missing his fun in the water, tell him that swimming is *never* safe during a storm.

Tips for Learning

Your time in the pool can be more enjoyable if you remember the following suggestions.

CLOTHES TO BRING

If your child is not potty trained, you may wonder how you will keep the water from being contaminated by urination and bowel movements. You can't prevent some contamination. After your child has been in the pool, turn on the filter and add extra chemicals.

You can prevent some accidents by dressing your child in *tight-fitting disposable diapers* covered by plastic pants. Take extra diapers and change them immediately after soiling occurs.

You may or may not want to cover the diapers with a bathing suit. A bathing suit can be binding, but you both may enjoy seeing how cute he looks

Bring warm, dry clothes for your child to wear after lessons.

in it. Make the bathing suit a part of the fun of being in the water. Say, ''Isn't it fun to have a colorful bathing suit like yours?''

OTHER THINGS TO BRING

Besides diapers, bring several towels to dry your child at the end of the lesson. Thorough drying is necessary to prevent chilling.

Bring sunscreen. If the sun is shining brightly, apply the sunscreen to your child's face and shoulders. You may have to repeat this during your time in the pool.

Many mothers pack a diaper bag with a bottle of milk or snack to give their child after the lesson. Take food if exercising in the water makes your youngster hungry.

Kickboard—This is an important teaching aid in the toddler program. You can buy one in most sporting-goods departments. Kickboards come in

Choose the correct-size kickboard for your child.

many colors, shapes and sizes. Choose one that is large enough to support your child. Be sure it is small enough for him to handle comfortably. Soft plastic or foam boards are better than hard ones.

Other Teaching Aids—Bring a pingpong ball when teaching your toddler to blow bubbles underwater. Take along a waterproof doll on the days you're teaching him submersion. Use of these tools is explained in the Toddler section.

During the more-advanced weeks of toddler training, your child will enjoy diving to the bottom to pick up a variety of submergible toys. Buy special toys for this purpose, or tie a fishing sinker to his favorite waterproof toys.

THINGS NOT TO BRING

Some things are more harmful than helpful to your child when it comes to teaching him water safety.

Flotation Devices—The greatest danger of flotation devices is that your child won't realize the device is holding him up. He may jump in the water without it and expect to float. The shock he experiences when he sinks to the bottom can cause him to panic.

Do not buy your child waterwings, arm floats or any other flotation device. He needs a realistic perception of how his body works in the water.

Nose Plugs, Ear Plugs—Don't buy these for your child. In his water-safety training, he learns to breathe out when he is underwater. When he is doing this correctly, he won't get water in his nose.

Ear plugs do not reduce ear infections. They can interfere with your communication with your child. If he can't hear your loving, enthusiastic voice, he can't fully benefit from his lessons.

Precautions

Before you begin lessons, let's review some important warnings about water. As we have emphasized earlier, no child is *ever* drownproof! We say this because many accidents can happen in the water.

Your child will enjoy diving for submergible toys.

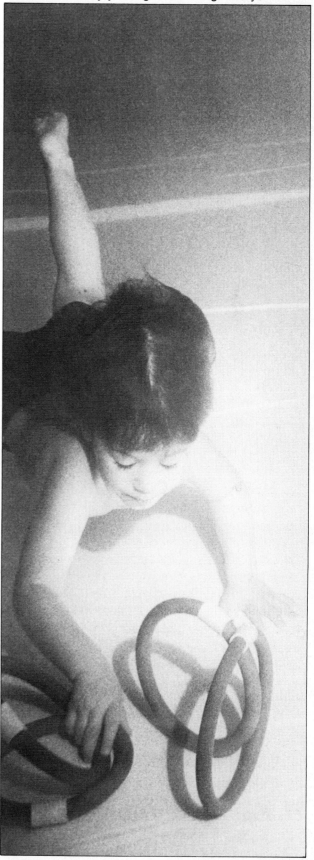

NEVER LEAVE HIM UNATTENDED

By following the instructions in this book, you can watersafe your child. But even if you feel certain your child is completely watersafe, never leave him unattended around *any* body of water.

Your child might bump his head on the pool edge, become entangled in a rope or fall in deep water. *An accident might make it impossible for him to reach the edge of the pool.*

Even the shock of falling in cold water can upset your child's reactions. Don't take a chance! Before you enter a pool, be sure you've taught your child to respect the water enough to stay away from it unless you are there.

As you teach your child in the pool, frequently repeat, "Johnny, never go near the water unless Mommy or Daddy is with you. Don't ever go near the edge of the pool by yourself!"

WATCH FOR TROUBLE SIGNS

Your child might be playing confidently in the water, but watch him constantly. Always be alert for signs of trouble.

Underwater Dangers—Keep a careful eye on your child when he is underwater. He can't breathe down there, so his life depends on your vigilance. Even when you think everything is fine, your child may be having problems. For example, you may think he is searching the bottom of the pool when he is lying there in trouble.

Never allow your child to stay underwater for more than 8 *seconds*. Even though he can hold his breath much longer, this is the longest period we consider safe. If your child does not come to the top by himself after being submerged for 5 seconds, go under and bring him up.

When teaching, don't submerge your child more than two times in a row. After that, take time out to play.

Bring him up after 5 seconds. Never submerge your child for more than 8 seconds maximum.

Always allow your child plenty of time to catch his breath between submersions. After he goes under the water once, he needs to fill his lungs with air before he goes under again.

Look for Bubbles—Make sure your toddler is blowing bubbles underwater. This lets you know he is holding his breath properly. If his bubbles become extra-large, he may be having problems. *Be responsive to this situation and bring him to the top immediately!*

An infant may not blow bubbles, but you can tell if he is holding his breath. If you look closely, you can see a small bubble of air in each nostril when he is underwater. Look for these bubbles. If you don't see them, bring your baby to the surface.

Swallowing Water—If your child doesn't close his mouth and hold his breath, he may swallow some pool water. Swallowing a small amount is normal and nothing to be alarmed about. The purification chemicals in a pool can't harm your child. Chemicals are so diluted he could never drink enough of them to affect his system.

If your child swallows water, he may wheeze, gag and spit some out. Don't be alarmed. Be sure he has a chance to get rid of all the water in his mouth before you submerge him again. Pat him on the back and remind him to close his mouth when he goes underwater.

Too much swallowed water can cause your child to get sick to his stomach. To keep this from happening, help him get rid of the water he has swallowed. Place him face-forward on your shoulder. Raise his buttocks up so his head is lower than his stomach and hanging down your back. The water he has swallowed will flow from his stomach out of his mouth.

Burping—This is caused when your child swallows air along with pool water. If you think your child needs to burp, stop the lesson and follow your usual burping procedures. You might also try pressing gently on his stomach.

Spitting Up—This happens when a burp forces a small amount of partially digested milk or food

When your child spits up or burps, follow your usual procedures.

from your child's stomach. Unless you think spitting up is going to turn into vomiting, continue with the lesson. Help your child clear his throat before he goes underwater.

Vomiting—If you schedule your child's lesson so he doesn't eat just before, vomiting should not be a problem. If your child begins to vomit, immediately take him out of the water! A vomiting child may breathe in some of the vomited material along with pool water. This can cause serious choking.

COMMON SENSE

At times your common sense will tell you to stop the lesson because your child seems overly tired or feverish. Don't let stubbornness or unrealistic goals keep you from following your own good judgment. Accidents happen most often during times of sickness or stress.

There are times when your common sense may tell you to skip the lesson entirely. If the water is too cold, for example, your blue-lipped, shivering child isn't going to learn much. Wait for a warmer day or find a heated pool.

Sickness is another reason to postpone your lesson. If your child has a communicable disease such as chicken pox, measles or impetigo, he should not go near the water. If he has a cold, sore throat or earache, he might get chilled in the water and make his condition worse.

Always check with your physician when your child is getting over an illness. Then you will know when it's safe to start lessons again.

LEARN CPR

We recommend every parent take a course on cardiopulmonary resuscitation. This is given by the Red Cross, fire stations, hospitals and qualified independent instructors.

A valuable guide to keep on hand to review these techniques is HPBooks' *How To Save a Life Using CPR,* by Lindsay Curtis. You'll learn what to do if your child needs resuscitation and gain the ability to save other lives. Here are the basic

Place your mouth over your child's mouth and nose to make a tight seal. Breathe at a rate of 1 breath every 3 seconds.

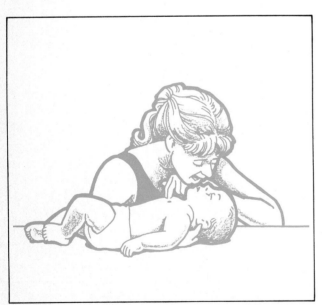

For infants, compress chest at a rate of 100 compressions per minute. Give 1 breath to every 5 compressions.

Take a deep breath. Open your mouth wide and place it over the infant's *mouth and nose* to make a tight seal. Breathe into his mouth and nose hard enough to make his chest rise. Continue rescue breathing at a rate of one breath every 3 seconds, or 20 times a minute.

If the infant does not begin breathing on his own, take his pulse at the artery located on the inside of his upper arm. If there is no pulse, use chest compression to artificially circulate his blood.

Bare the infant's chest. Put one hand under his upper body. Put *two fingers* of your other hand on the sternum between the nipples. Press the chest down 1/2 to 1 inch at a rate of 100 compressions per minute, or about two times per second.

Press five times, then give a rescue breath through the infant's mouth and nose. If you have a helper, he can give the rescue breaths for you. Continue in a regular rhythm until the infant starts breathing on his own or emergency help arrives.

CPR for Toddlers—Place the unconscious child flat on his back on a hard surface. Open the airway by lifting his chin and tilting his head back.

Place one hand under the child's neck to sup-

techniques of CPR for children. Study the illustrations as you read the instructions.

CPR for Infants—Place the unconscious infant flat on his back on a hard surface. Tilt his head back *gently*—never force it. Place one hand under his upper back to support an open airway.

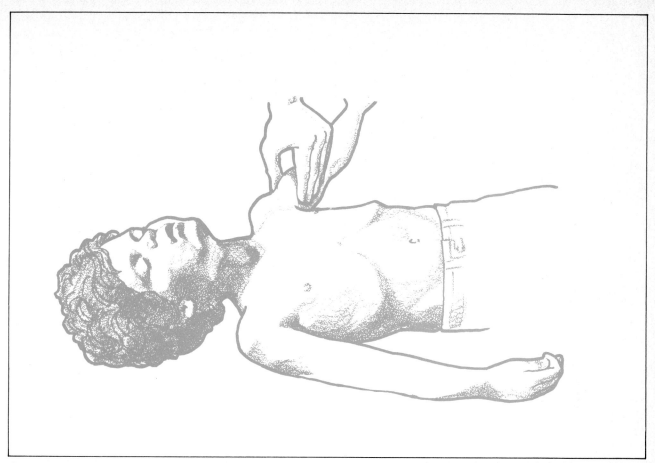

Check pulse at the artery at inside of upper arm.

port the open airway. Use the other hand to pinch his nostrils closed.

Take a deep breath. Open your mouth wide and place it over the child's mouth to make a tight seal. Breathe into his mouth hard enough to make his chest rise.

Give four quick, full breaths to fill his lungs. Take in fresh air between each breath you give. Continue rescue breathing at a rate of one breath every 4 seconds, or 16 times per minute.

If the child does not begin breathing on his own, take his pulse at the artery located on the inside of his upper arm. If there is no pulse, use chest compression to circulate his blood artificially.

Bare the toddler's chest. Put one hand under his neck. Put the palm of your hand on the sternum midway between the nipples. Press the chest down 3/4 to 1-1/2 inches at a rate of 80 to 100 compressions per minute, or about 1-1/2 times per second.

Press five times, then give a rescue breath through the child's mouth. If you have a helper, he can give the rescue breaths for you. Continue in a regular rhythm until the toddler starts breathing on his own or emergency help arrives.

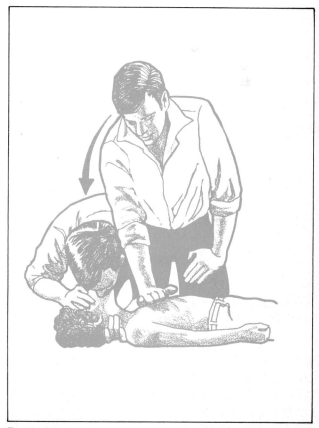

For toddlers, compress at a rate of 80 to 100 compressions per minute. Give 1 breath to every 5 compressions.

Your Child's Development

Your child's stage of development has a lot to do with the progress he makes in his water-safety training. For example, an infant up to 9 months old doesn't know how to use his muscles in a completely coordinated manner. For this reason, he is slower than a toddler when it comes to learning motor skills.

An infant has the advantage of having no acquired fears of the water. He reacts according to his instincts, and he trusts you. You may find it is easy to teach your infant water-survival techniques.

Younger toddlers usually do not learn motor skills as rapidly as older toddlers. Younger toddlers may take longer to complete the water-safety program. But older toddlers may have more fears to overcome before they feel comfortable in the water.

Every child is unique. Don't make general judgments about progress. Never compare your child's water-safety achievements with that of other children.

Be flexible in your expectations. Following are some age characteristics of infants and toddlers. But don't expect your son or daughter to develop exactly at this pace. Every child chooses the speed that's right for him.

Infants have not had time to acquire fear of water.

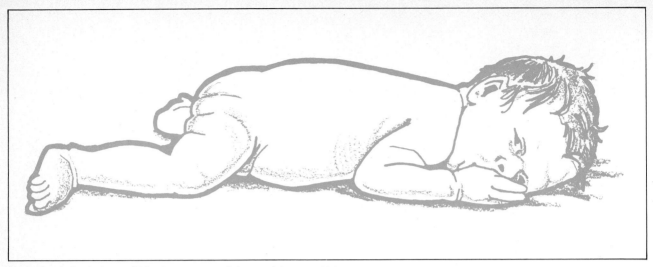

Your tiny infant shows little awareness of the world around him.

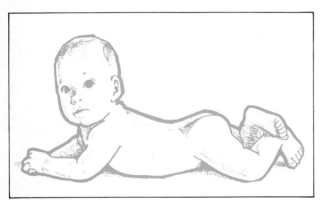

At 3 months, he turns his head and follows you with his eyes.

INFANTS

During his first year, your baby is dependent on you for nearly all his needs. Reinforce your bond of love through close physical contact.

Newborn to 6 Weeks—Your newborn's body is growing rapidly. He spends most of his time sleeping. He shows few personality responses or much awareness of the world around him.

6 Weeks—He can hold up his head and smile. Although he is somewhat nearsighted, he loves to stare at faces, especially yours.

6 Weeks to 3 Months—His vision is improving. He can follow a moving person with his eyes and stare at a bright object. In the bath or pool, he kicks his feet in the water.

3 Months—As your baby develops more strength in his hands and arms, he begins to reach out and grasp things. He turns his head freely to observe activities. He often rolls over in bed. When he is crying, he may be quieted by soothing music.

4 Months—Your baby splashes his hands in the water and raises them to reach for objects. When he is happy, he laughs out loud. He can now firmly hold toys.

5 to 6 Months—Your infant sits up by himself. He is becoming more alert. He turns his head at the sound of a voice or bell. You can tell he knows the difference between a stranger and a familiar person. He often objects when something is taken away from him. In the bathtub or pool, he coos and plays happily.

7 to 8 Months—Your baby is more active. He has begun to crawl around the house and is into everything. He may have temper tantrums and bang his spoon on his highchair tray. He's beginning to get a few teeth in his lower jaw.

YOUNGER TODDLERS

Your infant has become an independent little person with a mind of his own.

9 to 10 Months—Your infant can pull himself up and may already take a few steps on his own. He understands a lot of what you say. He tries to say words back to you. He gestures and waves bye-bye. When he's angry, he may throw things. Babies often become shy at this age.

10 to 12 Months—Your child may say his first words during this period. He is probably walking by himself. He's also beginning to climb. His shyness may increase, and he may show fear around strangers.

12 to 15 Months—Your child's walking ability is improving. If you laugh and encourage him, he will repeat his actions. At the table, he blows bubbles and drinks from a cup.

OLDER TODDLERS

Older toddlers have lots of energy. Your child is beginning to learn to control his behavior.

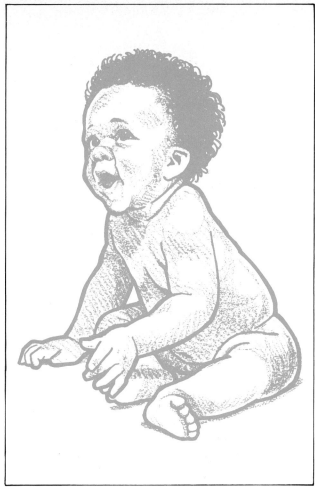

Your 6-month-old sits up by himself.

As he approaches 1 year, he learns to walk and say words.

15 to 18 Months—Your youngster helps you put on his clothes. He can stack up two or more building blocks. He uses a spoon in a messy way. His vocabulary grows each day.

18 Months to 2 Years—Your child can climb stairs and is always on the go. He scribbles on paper and turns the pages of a book. He uses short sentences and refers to himself by name. At the table, he eats with good control. He can build a high tower with blocks.

2 to 3 Years—Your growing toddler is usually happy and cheerful. He makes good sentences and understands much of what you say to him. He plays by himself and enjoys being with friends. He also feeds himself and has become bladder-and-bowel trained.

3 to 4 Years—Your toddler is developing a personality of his own. If you reward him with praise, he obeys simple instructions. He's learning at a rapid rate, but don't rush your child at this time. Let him set the pace.

Motor skills develop rapidly and the transition may be difficult.

Your infant has a growing memory.

Infants usually have a short attention span and quickly become bored if you repeat the same skill too much. Here's a good rule for teaching your infant: *Twice through and let that do—for now.*

INFANT MOTOR DEVELOPMENT

Infants follow a definite pattern of development. For instance, a baby normally learns to sit, crawl, stand and walk.

Physical development proceeds from the head to the feet. An infant first learns to control his head and neck muscles, then his arms and hands, then his torso, legs and feet.

Keep this head-to-feet sequence in mind as you train your child in water safety and survival. He needs to learn to use each muscle in a coordinated manner.

It takes more effort than adults realize for a baby to learn a new motor skill. When he finally learns a skill, you may notice him practicing it over and over again. Encourage him to do this.

TODDLER DEVELOPMENT

Toddlers acquire new motor skills faster than babies. They've learned to use their bodies, and they love to run and climb. The new skills they learn in the water bring them pleasure.

Toddlers also have a longer attention span than infants. But don't get pushy or impatient when teaching. You will soon recognize your child's preferred speed for learning. Your goal is to go rapidly enough to challenge him without frustrating him.

Don't forget to praise him often, hug him tightly, cuddle him and love him. You'll both succeed!

Learning Patterns

For many years people thought infants under 6 months old had little capacity for learning. Recent research suggests learning begins in the first few days of life. In fact, because of their inborn curiosity, babies may learn better at this stage than at any other time in their lives.

INFANT MENTAL DEVELOPMENT

At first infants don't make a connection between what they see and what they hear. They don't understand cause and effect. They do have a memory, though. A baby 3 to 6 months old has begun to file these memories in his mind and will be able to recall certain bits of information when needed.

By the time your infant is ready to learn water safety, he will have learned to make choices. He will know your face and love to stare at it. He will be curious about many things and will love to learn.

Communication Skills

You've been thinking about starting your child's water-safety training. He is at least 3 months old, and you've found a heated pool that's perfect for teaching.

Before you get in the water, think about an area that is closely related to your child's development—communication of thoughts and feelings. To be a good teacher, you must be a good communicator.

By the time your infant becomes a toddler, you will communicate by talking. But how can you communicate with an infant who can't understand what you say? There are many other ways to communicate than by talking. In the pool, you'll use all of them.

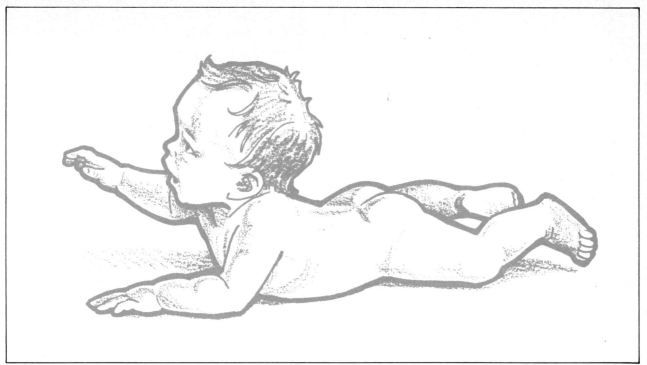
He first learns to control his head and neck muscles.

FACIAL MESSAGES

Your infant begins to see at birth. He is near-sighted at first, but his vision rapidly improves. He loves to stare at human faces and often smiles at them.

Soon your child can distinguish between different colors. He will even develop preferences for some colors over others. For instance, 4-month-old infants seem to prefer red and blue.

You will notice your baby's growing ability to follow you and your movements. He will constantly look for you to assure himself you are there.

Maintain Eye Contact—Always try to stay in your infant's view when you are in the pool. Keep your face above his so you have *direct eye contact*. Never wear dark sunglasses that block the eye messages you send.

When your baby looks in your eyes, he reads your moods and understands your responses to his activities. He knows if you approve of him or if you are displeased with him.

Your mood often becomes his mood, your attitude his attitude. Likewise, your enthusiasm becomes his enthusiasm, or your boredom becomes his boredom.

Smile, Laugh—At 3 months old, infants communicate their excitement with jerky movements of their arms and legs, as a dog does by wagging its tail. So get your baby moving by putting animation in your smile!

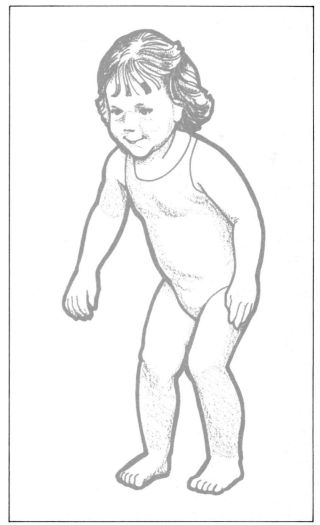
As your toddler matures, learning new water skills is fun.

Your Child's Development **27**

If your baby laughs, laugh with him. Laugh with your eyes, as well as your voice. Your infant quickly perceives your joy as he studies your eyes.

VOICE MESSAGES

Infants can hear before they are born. Living in the uterus is like living on a busy intersection. Your infant hears noisy bowel sounds and the blood that flows through your heart and blood vessels. Your speech, though muffled, can also be heard. So can noises like the hum of the dishwasher or the honk of a horn.

Loud sounds startle and soft sounds soothe. Rhythmical sounds may lull your unborn baby to sleep. After he is born, noises affect him the same way.

Music to His Ears—You may not have a beautiful voice, but your voice is music to your infant's ears. In his first few weeks, your baby learns to recognize your voice.

When teaching in the pool, keep up a steady stream of *patter* with your baby. Sing to him, hum to him, talk softly to him, reassure and praise him. Speak in a melodious, soothing tone, often in a whisper.

Repeat your infant's name. He loves to hear it. When you say his name, he knows you're talking to him.

Avoid Sudden, Loud Noises—Laugh frequently but not loudly, or you'll startle your infant. Loud, sudden noises can cause him to pucker up and cry, losing his confidence.

For this reason, *never* get angry when you are in the pool. Your baby will hear it in your voice and become afraid. Scolding, shouting and criticizing are out of place in this training.

Never try to teach a crying baby. Cuddle him and soothe him with soft, gentle sounds until he has calmed down and is happy again.

Talk to Your Toddler—The same gentle manner is important for teaching a toddler. Besides repeating his name and singing happy songs to him, give him verbal instructions for each new skill.

When giving your toddler instructions, speak slowly and distinctly so he understands you. Face him and maintain eye contact so you can fortify verbal instructions with eye messages and gestures. Laugh and smile as much as possible. Let him know that being in the water is fun!

TOUCH MESSAGES

The sense of touch is often neglected in our society as a way to communicate. Your infant learns many things when he feels your touch. He knows if you are angry, exasperated, impatient or bored. He can tell if you are overjoyed, excited or proud of him. No matter how hard you try, you can't hide the feelings expressed in your touch.

Until he masters floating, never leave your

Your baby will respond quickly to the way you treat him.

Your loving touch teaches many things.

Hum and talk softly to create a secure, happy mood.

baby unsupported in the water. Always give support and confidence with the gentle touch of your hand.

Enjoy this chance to cuddle and hold your infant as much as possible. Your hugs will make him love the water!

INFANT MESSAGES

Your infant's first communication is by crying and kicking. That's how he obtains the attention he wants and needs.

Infants try to talk from the day they are born. Studies reveal a newborn baby works his mouth along with his arms and legs when he hears his mother talking to him.

Talking in the Water—Your infant chuckles, laughs and squeals with delight when he is having fun with you in the pool. If he laughs, laugh with him. Try blowing on his tummy or humming in his ear. Watch him try to talk to you as you cuddle and squeeze him.

At 9 months old, your baby will babble as he tries to communicate with you. Acknowledge your baby's efforts to speak by talking back to him. Smile and tell him, "I agree. That's right! You've worked hard. Now let's play for a while."

Your baby will try to communicate with you.

Overcoming Fear

There are several things you can do to calm your child's anxieties when you are with him in the water.

INFANT FEARS

Your infant spends his first 9 months of life surrounded by warm water in the uterus. Unfortunately, he soon forgets how accustomed to water he once was.

He probably enjoys his bath, so make this a pleasant time of day. Sing and talk to him. Encourage him to kick and splash his hands in the water. In this way, you can begin his water-safety training before you enter the pool.

Fear of Deep Water—By the time he is 9 months old, your toddler will recognize the difference between the deep and shallow ends of the pool. He may develop some fear of the deep end.

There is no reason for you to go into deep water. Teach by the steps of the pool at a depth of about 42 inches. What is shallow water to you is deep water to your infant!

Calm your infant's fear of deep water when you enter the pool. Make your entrance gradual, filled with soothing words. Wait on each step until your baby becomes accustomed to the deeper water.

By the time he is 9 months old, your baby may fear the deep end.

Hold your infant securely during your first moments in the pool. As the lesson progresses, gradually relinquish some of this hold. You must judge how much your baby needs the sense of security that your arms provide.

Always keep your baby's face out of the water during his introduction to the pool. If you play splashing games, make the splashes tiny and gentle. Sing and laugh and make it fun.

Fear of Loud Noises—This fear is instinctive. All babies are born with it.

We have discussed the importance of finding a quiet, uncrowded pool for teaching your infant. Your talking, singing and humming provide a positive hearing experience for your infant's ears.

If a loud noise scares your infant, hum or sing to him until he is happy again. Schedule your lessons at a time of day when traffic noises and other distractions are at a minimum.

Fear of Falling—Your child may show this instinctive fear when you try to teach him to float on his back. In your infant's mind, "lying back" is similar to falling. Until he becomes used to it, it will cause him to feel insecure. His response to this insecurity is tension and resistance to teaching.

The upright position is the position to start with when you take your infant in the pool. Hold him securely against your chest and shoulders, as you do when burping him. Later, you can hold him in the cradle position with your hands firmly under his head and buttocks. He's on his back, but he feels secure.

The feeling of being supported is important to your infant. When he feels your arms firmly cradling his back, he has no fear of falling. Eventually, you will remove this support so he can float freely on his own. Do this slowly and tenderly so your baby scarcely notices your arms are gone. *Never remove support from his body suddenly!*

Fear of Submersion—When you begin teaching submersion, your infant may cry at the first sensation of water in his eyes, ears or nose. Don't worry—he quickly learns to close his mouth and hold his breath. Because his fear of going underwater is not instinctive, you can help him overcome it.

Signs of Fear—Be alert to what your baby is trying to communicate when he whimpers or cries. Try to sense when apprehension begins. Don't let it develop into fear. Don't be so intent on making progress that you overlook what your child is trying to tell you.

Be patient. Slow down when necessary. Take time to praise, love, hug and reassure your child.

Until he becomes used to the position, your child may feel insecure on his back.

Be alert to signs of terror.

If the lesson isn't fun for your infant, stop and play with him.

To overcome his feeling of fear, support and soothe your baby. There's no rush. Enjoy your infant in the water!

SIGNS OF TERROR

Usually a terrified infant or toddler is having a negative experience. Check to see if you have been pushing him too fast or expecting too much from him. The water experience may be losing its fun and becoming unpleasant.

A terrified child has difficulty communicating. He may cry uncontrollably or become silent and withdrawn. He may whimper constantly, even when being pulled around on a kickboard.

Physical Signs—Look for a terrified facial expression. Besides this sign, check for rigid arms and legs, or extreme limpness. Some terrified children shiver uncontrollably, even in warm water. Their lips turn blue and their breathing becomes shallow.

What to Do—Slow down and stop pushing your child. Allow him to take longer, if this is what he requires.

Review your techniques of teaching to see if you are supporting his body adequately. You may be withdrawing your support too suddenly or too completely. Never take away your supporting hand until he's had the chance to develop security in the skill you are teaching him. Check to see if you are submerging your child too often or too long. Allow him to get his breath.

Don't Give Up—Once you help your child overcome his terror, go on with the project or exercise. Readjust and start over, but don't allow your child to fail. Just take more time.

Play with your infant or toddler in the water, but don't take him out of the pool because he cries. Talk to him soothingly, lovingly and patiently until he quiets down. Give him plenty of hugs, but don't allow him to cling.

FEARS TODDLERS HAVE

The things that make a toddler more mature mentally are the things that may make him fearful of the water. He may have had a bad experience with water and remember it. He can imagine things in the future and may worry about drowning. He knows the water is dangerous. Until he becomes watersafe, a pool is a threat to him.

Get your toddler to talk about his fears. Try to calm them one by one. Let him know that you're going to be with him all the time he's in the pool.

As you enter the water, go slowly and hold his hand or hug him. Keep the water out of his face.

Once you're in the pool, stay close to him. If he seems fretful, maintain a loving hold on him during the lesson.

Eventually, even the most anxiety-prone toddler begins to notice the special attention he is getting. He starts to participate actively in the games and songs. Soon he forgets his fears and feels happy and secure in the water.

Fun Overcomes Fear—If you have fun teaching your child, he will have fun learning from you. Spend plenty of time in the pool playing as well as teaching. Always make the atmosphere one of happiness, confidence and love. Your teaching can be so concealed by fun your child won't realize he is being trained in water safety and survival.

YOUR FEARS

If you are afraid of water, it is difficult to hide your fear from your child. Because of this, you may want to take a swimming course before you begin training your infant or toddler. If you have fears you can't overcome, it may be best to have your spouse or someone else teach your child.

Your attitudes are mimicked by your infant or toddler. He will grow up liking foods you like, developing opinions patterned after yours and learn-

Don't allow your child to cling to you. Independence is important in our water-safety program.

ing the fears you have. If you are afraid of the water, your infant or toddler will be, too.

This may be the best time for you to get rid of your own fears. The power of love and reassurance can overcome apprehension and anxiety. Love should be abundant when you are training your child in the water. Because you love and care so much, you may be able to overcome fear in yourself and your child!

Your child will reflect your fears.

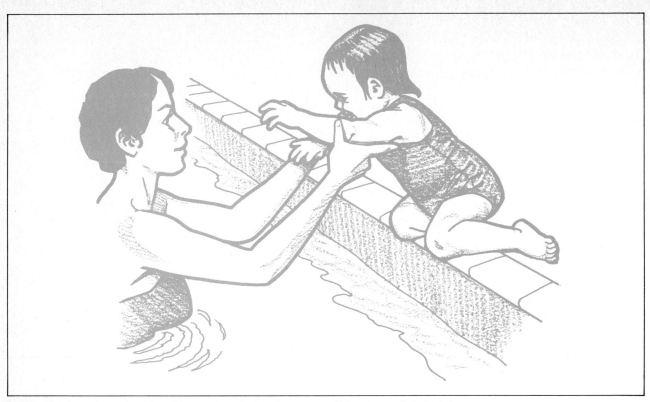

Motivation is an important teaching tool and a key to successful water-safety training.

Praise your child as you cuddle and hug her.

Motivating Your Child

Motivation is important in any teaching situation. As you work with your child, you will find motivation is one of the keys to his success. You must make him *want* to learn, and there are many ways you can do this.

Don't push your child too hard. That isn't motivation. Your child won't realize you are trying to help him learn a life-saving skill. He'll realize you are demanding, and he may rebel. Try to make the lessons fun and interesting. Keep him involved and enjoying the water. Praise and encourage him to motivate him into trying new things.

If your child is a toddler, you can make a chart, using the achievement scorecard on page 89. Write each skill on a separate line. When he masters a skill, put a star on the chart. This visual measure of his success can motivate him to earn more stars.

A younger child will not understand that kind of motivation. You will have to provide loving encouragement and praise for a job well done. Your child will be motivated to earn your praise and keep trying.

Motivation must always be *positive*. If you act negatively with your child, you will not motivate him. If you demand more than he can do, you will create problems. Give your child love and reassurance, and he'll respond.

REWARDS FOR YOUR CHILD

Motivating your infant or toddler to learn the exercises necessary for water safety and survival is one of the keys of this program. You are going to have to tempt him with rewards. Rewards are not bribes. Bribes are given for illegal or unjustified action. Rewards are earned. The best rewards your child will want to earn are fun, approval and your example.

Reward of Fun—If you can make the lessons *fun* for him, your child will be willing and eager to do whatever you want him to do. When the exercises cease to be fun, your child will drag his feet and resist you.

You may have to spend the majority of every lesson on fun things to get him to accept a few minutes of effective instruction. Again we repeat the primary rule of this teaching method—always allow enough time to play in the water. Spend time having fun.

Infant games can be simple and silly. Blow bubbles on your baby's tummy and play peek-a-boo. Tow him around like a boat.

Bouncing is another favorite activity. This is how you comfort your baby, even when he's out of water—by bouncing him gently up and down. Bounce him on top of the water until he is happy and cooing, then turn in a circle. Bouncing is the best way to calm your baby if he becomes frightened in the water.

Toddler games can be more structured. You already know games that delight your child. Use your imagination to change them slightly so they can be played in the water.

Try hiding small objects on the steps or under your feet. Your toddler will love to hunt for them. Or play tag games that get him moving in the water.

A child enjoys being pulled around on a kickboard. Let him pretend he's a motorboat and have him make appropriate noises. Use the kickboard to play a game of "fetch." Shove the board away from you and have your child bring it back,

Laughter is a wonderful reward.

kicking to propel himself as you have taught him.

Have your toddler wrap his legs around your waist. Turn around in a circle as you sing to him. Try playing simple infant games like bouncing and towing. Your toddler isn't too old to enjoy these.

Reward of Approval—One of the most enticing things you can use with your child is your approval of his actions. After any amount of progress, repeat often, "Oh, Bobby, you did so well! You grabbed the wall! I'm so proud of you!" As you hug him say, "Bobby, I love you so much!"

When the lesson is over and you are drying your child with a towel, offer more hugs and approval. Say, "Joey, we had a wonderful time today. You're doing so well and having so much fun!"

No matter how often you say these words to your child he never tires of them. Whenever you can, applaud him.

Reward of Example—Another reward for your child is your own example. If you are teaching him to blow bubbles, you blow bubbles. Submerge when he submerges. This is called the *power of example*. Your infant or toddler wants to copy you.

An older sibling who knows how to swim can provide another good example. Your child wants to imitate his "grown-up" brother or sister.

Vary the games you play with your child in the water.

Every infant or toddler has a drive to develop new skills. In a supportive environment, his skills increase and improve every day. There is no better stimulation than a good example for him to follow.

Children are master imitators. Besides imitating things you do in the water, your child will often mirror your mood. Bubble with enthusiasm. You can say, "Patti, that was great the way you grabbed the wall!" Or try flattering her with praise like, "Isn't it fun to go swimming and wear a pretty swimsuit like yours?"

Material Rewards—Some parents like to reward their child with food treats or trinkets when he performs a new skill in the water. We strongly recommend against this practice.

Candy and cookies can make a child burp, vomit or choke in the water. Hard foods like popcorn or peanuts can be sucked into his lungs. Coins and small toys can be swallowed. They are also distracting. Your child may show more interest in them than in his lesson.

Fun, approval and your own enthusiastic example are the three best rewards you can offer your child. Save the cookies and toys for after the lesson.

Use the power of example to teach skills like blowing bubbles.

OTHER TEACHING TIPS

Your skill as a teacher is fully developed when you can guide your child through an exercise so he doesn't realize he's being taught. But motivating devices can't do the job by themselves. Sometimes you must be strict.

Firm Expectations—Infants and toddlers often love to take a bath, but many of them hate to have their hair washed. When your child's hair is dirty, you let him know he must have his hair washed. He knows nothing will change your mind—even crying won't help. If your child is like this, you have already learned the secret of *firm expectations.*

At certain points in your child's water-safety training, you are going to have to "wash his hair." You must make progress, and he must learn.

Let your child know you have firm expectations. No amount of crying will make you take him out of the water. He will learn the skill, and you will teach him. Do the job with love, but *do it.*

Sing to Success—Some mothers sing a certain song before they wash their child's hair. This lets the child know what is about to happen and what is expected of him. Use this same trick in the pool with your child.

Your child may not like to have his hair washed, but when you're firm, you get the job done.

Provide plenty of physical guidance when you work with your child in the water.

Infants and toddlers have difficulty shifting their attention rapidly from one activity to another, especially if they are supposed to concentrate on the activity. For this reason, use a special song before a particular activity.

Your child soon identifies each new water-safety skill with the song associated with it. When you start to sing the tune, he'll soon perform the skill for you without thinking.

Make up tunes that are special for you and your child. Or slightly change tunes your child already likes by substituting the word *kick* for *run, splash* for *dance,* and so forth. The songs in the box on page 43 will give you some ideas. These are favorites with the infants and toddlers in our program. They love to sing and move to them.

Physical Guidance—As a parent, you know what motivates your child. You probably have your own special words of praise. You know how to caress and hug him in ways he enjoys.

You also know how to distract your youngster by talking to him about other things. You have discovered he is uncomfortable with many things that are strange to him until he is used to them. Then he probably enjoys them.

You must often physically guide your child through a new procedure to help him learn it. He may resist physical guidance at first, so fill it with love.

Physical guidance is always necessary when you begin to teach each new water-safety skill. Instead of long explanations or attempts at persuasion, use your hands to move your child through the water.

As lessons proceed, keep up this physical assistance. If your child doesn't follow your instructions, guide his head, arms, legs or body through the required motions.

Your touch should be gentle but firm, sensitive but solid. You can gradually lighten it as your child learns to perform each new skill on his own. You will soon be able to let up completely on physical guidance and watch your child take over.

Example—One situation that calls for physical guidance often occurs. When you are teaching your child to swim to the wall and grab hold, he may turn around and try to cling to you instead of the wall. If he does this, quickly turn his body while he is still underwater so he faces the wall. Give him a slight push on his buttocks so he glides to the wall and grasps the edge by himself.

Physical guidance can replace explanations and arguments. Never permit your child to direct the lesson or interrupt it. Quickly and quietly guide

Firm, gentle physical guidance replaces arguments.

him through the exercise, then praise him for having done it. He rapidly learns to do as you direct, so he can win approval.

MOTIVATING YOUR SPECIAL CHILD

We have never liked the term *handicapped.* Some children are *special* with special problems. They seem to have other ways of overcoming these problems.

Think Success—Your mentally or physically handicapped child can successfully learn water safety and survival. Because his life is filled with challenges, he knows how to handle the challenges of the water.

In our program, we have successfully taught youngsters without legs. Cerebral-palsy victims who have little control over their muscles have been good students. All share one valuable characteristic—they are determined to learn and succeed in their own special ways.

Consult your child's physician before you begin his water-safety training. Find out what precautions you must take when dealing with his handicap in the water. Careful preparation will ensure success.

Case Histories—Two-year-old Nicholas had encephalitis that left him severely brain-damaged. When he began the water-safety course, he could not speak. His actions were jerky and uncoordinated.

Nicholas learned all the skills in the program. He is now communicating well and attending preschool. Everyone is surprised and delighted by his progress.

Praise every step of progress, no matter how small it is.

Four-year-old Rebecca is a cerebral-palsy child. When she first entered the pool, every movement resulted in hyperactive flailing. Eventually, Rebecca was able to master all the techniques. Now she is learning to race in the water.

Two-year-old Lila has Down's Syndrome. Her teacher says since the little girl learned water safety, her progress in every area of learning has improved.

Self-Confidence—Children like Nicholas, Rebecca and Lila have successfully learned water safety because their parents believed they *could* learn. Begin by building your child's self-esteem. Stress his importance as an individual. Focus on what he *can do,* not on what he can't do.

Remove negative words from your vocabulary. Never say *can't, hopeless, failure* or *quit*. Instead say, "David, you *can* do it! I know you can!"

With your loving encouragement, your child's desire to succeed helps him reach his goal.

Praise every step of progress, no matter how small it may be. Applaud his efforts, not just his achievements. Trying may cost him a tremendous amount of energy. His sincere attempt to learn is a success in itself.

End every teaching session on a positive note. Praise and cuddle your child as you dry him with a towel. Your praise and love are his well-earned rewards.

Show Your Love—Treat your child with affection, tolerance and compassion. Everything you do in the pool should show your child how much you love him. Express your love in the tenderness of your touch and the warmth of your voice. Your special child responds by doing his best to please you.

Disregard Your Calendar—Don't set goals in terms of days, weeks or months. Let your child set the pace that's right for his physical and mental abilities.

Practice each exercise many times. Your youngster will master the skill if you give him enough time. Never push, and don't become discouraged. You and your special child will succeed together!

RULES OF MOTIVATION

Follow these five rules as you instruct your child in the water:

1. Motivate your child with rewards of fun, approval and your own example.
2. Have firm expectations. Don't let the child's reluctance interfere with the progress of instruction.
3. Sing a certain song when you introduce each new skill. Your child soon identifies that song with the skill. He will perform the skill when he hears you start to sing.
4. Provide physical guidance immediately when your child does not follow your instructions.
5. Be patient and loving with your child.

Remember motivation as you teach your child. If you reward him, he'll follow where you lead. And you'll both have fun along the way.

Behavior Problems

Have you ever seen a frustrated mother lose her temper with a toddler in public? The louder the child yells, the louder the mother yells, and the harder the toddler gets spanked. Avoid this kind of behavior when teaching your child in the pool.

Most of us are tolerant of temper tantrums in children. It is normal for a child to have a tantrum. Usually, the infant or toddler lets you know he doesn't want to learn anything. He kicks, screams and struggles as he tries to get out of the water. How *you* respond is important.

WHAT NOT TO DO

When your child is having a tantrum in the pool, what you don't do may be more important than what you do. Keep these simple rules in mind, and the screams and tears will stop.

● Don't lose your temper. If you do, you are no more mature than your child.
● Don't raise your voice. He will only cry louder, and you may lose control of yourself.
● Don't argue with him. This puts you on the same level as your child and tells him you are willing to debate the issue. A toddler who is having a temper tantrum is incapable of reasoning.
● Don't overreact. Babies and toddlers imitate. The more excited you become, the more excited your child becomes.
● Don't "shush" him. It doesn't work, and it makes him more upset.
● Don't sympathize with him. This learning experience is necessary to make him watersafe.
● Don't allow him to cling to you. Support him securely, but hold him at a distance. Face him away from you, so he can't cling. Continue with the lesson.
● Don't take him out of the water unless he seems terrified, cold or sick. If you do, you concede defeat.

WHAT TO DO

Here are some things to do when your child is misbehaving:

● Relax. You're not hurting your child physically or psychologically. Ignore his tantrums and behavior. Act as if you don't hear his cries.
● Talk and play with him or praise him. Otherwise, he might try to convince you to take him out of the water. Keep him in the pool and continue with the exercise.
● Be friendly and fair, but firm, consistent and loving. Your rules are like fences that your child must not cross. Let him know how far he can go. Once he knows the limits of his behavior, his exploration is over.
● If your toddler continues with his tantrum, lovingly lift him up, look him straight in the eye and say, "I will not accept that type of behavior." Put him back in the water and continue with your usual enthusiasm. This tactic may seem overly simple, but we have tried it with thousands of crying toddlers, and it works.
● Be patient and gentle with an infant who is having a tantrum. Telling him to stop isn't effective with a baby, so go back to the basics. Hug him, soothe him and gently bounce him on top of the water until his crying stops. But keep him in the water. Like a toddler, an infant must be shown you are a no-nonsense teacher.
● If your child's tantrum won't stop, continue the floating or kicking activity for another 5 minutes, then get out of the pool. Don't reward bad behavior by playing or allowing him to do what he wants. If he misbehaves, he misses play time.

Be patient and gentle with your infant when he is frightened or having a tantrum.

TODDLER'S POINT OF VIEW

Your child can't think like you, but he has feelings. Try to see things from his standpoint, and you will understand a lot about his behavior.

Watch your toddler when he's sitting on your lap. He explores your ears, eyes and hair, then suddenly begins to look up your nose. His fascination with your nostrils reveals an interesting fact—your toddler has an entirely different view of the world than you do. How would you like to see most people as they look from under their chins?

When you are in the water, try to see the pool from your child's point of view. Think in his terms of distance. See things from his eye level.

PATIENCE COUNTS

Be patient. The first few weeks are always the most difficult. Eventually your child will begin to enjoy the water.

Children are not basically misbehavers. They have either had a bad example or have not been directed into good behavior.

Establish your expectations early with your child and he will be a willing pupil. Be generous with your praise and love, but remember the purpose of the training. And don't forget to have fun together along the way.

WATERPLAY SONGS

For *Arm-Paddle*
Row, row, row your boat,
Gently down the stream,
Merrily, merrily, merrily, merrily,
Life is but a dream.

For *Back-Float*
A
London Bridge is falling down, falling down,
falling down,
London Bridge is falling down,
My fair lady!
Take the keys and lock 'em up, lock 'em up,
lock 'em up,
Take the keys and lock 'em up,
My fair lady!
Build it up with sticks and stones, sticks
and stones, sticks and stones,
Build it up with sticks and stones,
My fair lady!

B
Motorboat, motorboat, go so slow,
Motorboat, motorboat, go so fast,
Motorboat, motorboat, step on the gas!

C
Bluebells, cockleshells, eavie-ivy-over!
(repeat many times)

For *Flutter-Kick* on the kickboard

Here we go loup-t-lou,
Here we go loup-t-lie,
Here we go loup-t-lou,
All on a Saturday night.

For *Water Bouncing* games

I put my right foot in,
I take my right foot out,
I put my right foot in,
And I shake it all about.
I put my left foot in,
I take my left foot out,
I give my left foot a kick
and I turn myself about!

Infant Program

This section is designed for children up to the age of 9 months. If your baby is 9 months to 1 year old, you may find these techniques helpful, but the Toddler section should be your main guide. If he is more than 1 year old, go to the Toddler section.

We divided this section into progressive skills. Every infant learns at his own pace. Many babies complete the course in two weeks. Others take more or less time to master the skills. You know your baby's speed of learning. Respect it and you'll have success.

Teach the skills in the sequence they are presented, but don't be too rigid. If your baby balks at one step of the training, go to something else. Return to the other skill later. Review each skill several times during each lesson, even if your child seems to know it. The most important rule of this method is to intersperse work with play. Spend time having fun!

SUBMERSION

The first water-safety skill your infant learns is to hold his breath underwater.

Blow on His Face—Gradually accustom your infant to the water. Then make a game of blowing on his face. Hold him upright with your hands firmly beneath his armpits. Blow strongly in the direction of his nose and mouth.

Your infant squints, then inhales sharply. This is an instinctive reaction you will make use of in teaching. Practice blowing in his face several times above water.

After his sharp inhalation, your child holds his breath for a moment. Then he blows out the air he has inhaled. This is the safest time to bring his face below the surface. When he is holding his breath or blowing out, he cannot suck in water.

Under You Go—When you feel confident about blowing into your infant's face to produce the inhale response, proceed to submersion. Ideally,

Make a game of blowing in your child's face.

You will see bubbles as your child's nose goes underwater.

you submerge with your baby, maintaining eye contact all the time. Babies instinctively keep their eyes open underwater. Seeing your familiar face calms your child's fears.

Don't be afraid. This won't hurt your baby. Blow in his face, listen for the inhale and *keep on blowing!* Squat down to bring both of your faces below the surface of the water. Do this in one smooth movement. Keep your baby in the *upright* position.

Don't stay down for more than 5 seconds! When you come up, greet your infant with a big grin and hug.

Submerge several times in a lesson, but never more than twice in a row. Too many repetitions can make your baby bored and fussy.

He Can Do It Alone—If you don't feel comfortable about submerging yourself, you can still teach this skill to your baby. Hold him upright in front of you and blow in his face. Gently lower his body into the water, blowing constantly until his face goes below the surface.

If your baby is exhaling properly, you will see him blow bubbles as his nose goes underwater. Leave him underwater for 5 seconds. When you bring him up, grin and hug him.

Gagging, Sputtering—Until he learns to hold his breath underwater, your baby may breathe in some water. If he does this through his mouth, he'll probably swallow some water. When he comes up, he may gag and sputter. This is natural.

Let your infant regain control of his breathing

Let your infant catch his breath before you go under a second time.

before you go underwater again. Play the blowing game above the surface a few times to make sure he's inhaling sharply.

Soon your baby takes your blowing as a signal he's going underwater. He learns it's more comfortable when he holds his breath or exhales underwater. When he learns this, you can stop blowing in his face.

Many infants learn to hold their breath in only a few lessons. Others take longer. Don't stop blowing in your child's face until you're sure he holds his breath while he's underwater.

ASSISTED GLIDE TO THE WALL

Keep practicing submersion in every lesson. When your baby can hold his breath underwater, move to the next skill to learn the assisted glide to the wall.

Stand in the shallow end of the pool, about 5 feet from the wall. With your hands firmly under his armpits, move your infant onto his tummy in a horizontal swim position.

Slowly and calmly remove your hands from your infant's armpits. Allow him to float freely *for only a second or two!*

With your hands under his armpits, move your infant onto his tummy in the horizontal swim position.

Allow him to float freely for only a second or two.

Hold your baby firmly under the armpits, then relax and let go.

Stand by to give assistance as you glide him to the wall.

At first you may feel nervous about letting go of your infant. Relax and do it! Your baby won't learn if you don't let him go.

Glide to the Wall—Stand in the water, 5 feet from the wall. Stand on the left side of your infant. Place him on his tummy in the horizontal swim position with your hands under his armpits.

Release your baby and allow him to float freely for 3 or 4 seconds. Then place your hands on his buttocks at the hip joints and glide him carefully to the wall. He may need your assistance to grab the wall and hold on. If you have to help him, curve his hands over the coping of the wall, then place your hands over his. Repeat the entire exercise four or five times.

As you repeatedly glide your baby to the wall, you condition him to go there by himself every time he enters the water. If he accidentally falls in the water, he won't panic and turn toward the middle—he'll head for the wall.

GRASPING THE WALL

The ultimate goal of this water-safety program is to teach your infant to kick-glide to the wall, grasp it and hold on. He will automatically lift his head to take a breath. Start teaching him the grasping skill during the first few days of training.

Grasping Instinct—During his first months of life, your baby showed a grasping reflex. When you touched his palm with your finger, his fingers tightened around it.

Now that he is older, this reflex has disappeared. But your baby still instinctively clutches for your hair and reaches for toys. When you try to take something away from him, you know how strong his grasp can be.

Modify Instinct—You are going to modify your infant's instinct to reach for things and hold onto them. Through physical guidance and frequent repetition, you will teach him to grasp the pool wall.

When your child is comfortable in the upright position, squat down or move into deeper water.

When you glide your baby to the wall, release him for 3 or 4 seconds. Practice this activity several times. Then gently place your hands at his hips and lift him to grasp the wall. He will hold on. If he fails to grasp the edge, guide his hands to it and place your hands over his. This helps him learn to hold on.

After he curves his hands around the edge of the pool, support his buttocks with your knee. Brace his back with the front of your body. Let him practice grasping the side of the wall while you support him. After he has a firm grasp on the wall, he will automatically lift his head to take a breath of air. A newborn baby might not do this, but most babies 3 months old or older will grasp on to the edge and hold on.

If you practice this exercise often, your baby will learn to hold the edge. Keep your repetitions down to two in a row, but do it frequently.

ASSISTED BACK-FLOAT

Stand in water that's shoulder deep. If you are in shallower water, squat down to shoulder level. Hold your infant with his back toward you. Sing and play with him until he rests his head on your shoulder. The lower part of his body should be extended vertically in the water, and his legs will rise to the surface. Let him enjoy the experience.

Move to Horizontal Position—When your child is relaxed and comfortable in the upright position on your shoulder, *slowly* squat down or move to deeper water. Keeping his head on your shoulder, gradually ease his torso into the horizontal position. Sing to him and play with him until he's comfortable and confident.

When you feel the time is right, slowly ease his head down from your shoulder. Put one hand under his buttocks and the other under his head. If he tenses up and begins to cry, move him back up on your shoulder to cuddle him again.

Allow him to relax in the *horizontal back-float position* as you slowly walk around the pool. Sing and talk to him in a soothing manner. Try to get him to stretch out his arms so they are supported by the water. Keep his tummy up and his legs straight. His outstretched legs will naturally rise to the surface. This is the ideal back-float position.

Bouncing Exercise—For variety, hold your baby so he's facing you with his legs wrapped around your waist. Slowly lower his back into the water and support it with your hands. Bounce your baby through the water, first up and down, then turn in circles. Gradually lower your child into the water as you bounce him a little deeper each

If your child tenses up and begins to cry, ease her back up on your shoulder until she is happy again.

time. If you are careful not to frighten your baby or submerge his face, he will enjoy this exercise.

The bouncing exercise can also be done in the cradle position. Or try it in the horizontal back-float position, with or without your baby's head on your shoulder. Always keep your bouncing movements slow. Progress gradually from bouncing to other activities. Avoid sudden movements that startle or frighten your child.

Common Problems—At first your baby may not like being on his back. He feels unsupported, and this triggers his instinctive fear of falling.

Some infants arch their backs, and their heads go underwater. Some babies try to sit up. Other infants flail their arms or raise their legs, and many of them cry.

If your baby does any of these things, ease him back up on your shoulder. Bounce him and sing to him. Don't rush. Soon he'll feel relaxed enough to float comfortably in the water.

The bouncing exercise can also be done in the horizontal back-float position, with or without your child's head on your shoulder.

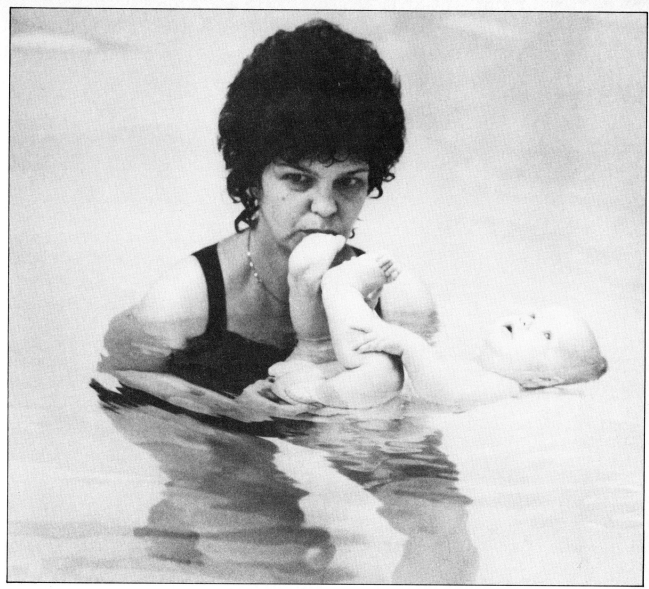

Some infants try to sit up or raise their legs. This can cause their face to go under the water.

SIT-DIVE

Your baby should be more accustomed to the water by now, although he may not be too happy about submersion and the assisted back-float. His attitude will improve as he gains confidence. Repeat the skills you have already introduced before going on to the sit-dive from the side.

Like an Accident—This exercise is designed to accustom your baby to the sensation of falling in the water. You're going to teach him not to panic if he accidentally falls in a pool.

Review the assisted glide to the wall several times before starting the sit-dive. The gliding exercises reacquaint your baby with the horizontal swim position and the feeling of being on his own in the water.

Use Your Hands—Help your child sit on the edge of the pool. Stand in the water facing him. Hold both of his hands, and put your right hand behind his head, if necessary.

Pull your baby directly down in the water so his arms and head enter first. Let him glide about 3 feet. He is underwater on his stomach in the horizontal swim position. You are still close to the wall.

While he is underwater, grasp your baby by his waist and temple. Rapidly turn him around so he faces the wall and you. Allow him to kick-glide back to the wall and grasp the edge. Help him with a push on his buttocks, if necessary. He will automatically lift his head for a breath of air.

Praise your baby when he performs the exer-

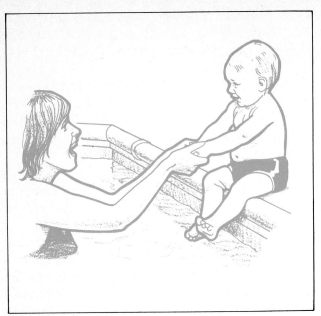

To teach the sit-dive, sit your infant on the pool edge and hold both his hands in yours.

Pull him into the water, head and arms first.

If your infant cannot sit up on her own, place her on her tummy at the edge of the pool.

cise. It's a big step for him and he deserves applause. Repeat this several times each lesson. Soon your baby will be able to do it on his own. After your baby accomplishes this exercise, praise him as you cuddle and hug him.

Because you are both in this exercise together, your baby responds positively and learns. He knows you are there and feels secure, especially when you hold him.

If your baby is crying when he comes up, wait until he is happy again before you repeat the sit-dive from the side. Because it's important, repeat it four times each lesson until your child masters it.

Variation—If your infant is too young to sit up confidently, place him on his tummy at the edge of the pool. Support his chest and buttocks with your hands as they extend over the water.

Propel your baby into the water with a boost from your hand on his buttocks. Turn him around and glide him back to the wall, as explained on page 53.

Common Problems—If at first your baby doesn't head toward you and the wall, reach out and physically turn him around with your hands. If he seems panicky or is swallowing water, bring him to the surface immediately.

One of the most common problems with this exercise involves the mother, not the child. She is scared to pull her baby into the water and let him kick-glide to the wall without her help.

If you feel this way, relax and reassure yourself. You are not hurting your baby. Resist the temptation to grab him and pull him toward you and the wall. This exercise is like learning to walk. He will never learn unless you let him do it on his own.

Propel her into the water with a boost on her buttocks.

Your toddler will soon kick-glide to the wall by himself.

Submerge to see if he is holding his breath or blowing out.

Bicycling—Some children do not propel themselves horizontally. They *bicycle* in a vertical position in their hurry to get to the surface. It is like treading water. If your child does this, correct him by submerging yourself about 24 inches below his body. You should be almost directly under his body. Move slowly backward while you are submerged. Your child will move to the horizontal position as he looks down at your face and kicks above you.

It is important to teach your child not to bicycle.

It won't propel him to the side of the pool. Eventually, bicycling exhausts him and he will give up. After overcoming the bicycling problem, allow him to propel himself 8 to 10 feet, then repeat several times.

KICK-GLIDE TO THE WALL

It may take days or weeks to master this phase of training, so don't rush your baby. Be patient and take it a step at a time. As you move your baby in the horizontal position toward the wall, hold him under his armpits for a one-two count. Release him for the count of three-four. If he needs an assist, lift him at the hips so he can grasp the side of the pool. Gradually increase the time he floats freely without your support.

If necessary, boost your baby on the buttocks to push him toward the wall. He will get the idea and kick-glide to the wall himself. When he can cover a 5-foot distance on his own, he has mastered the kick-glide to the wall. Reward him with hugs and praise.

Submerge to Check Progress—When your baby can kick-glide on his own for several feet, submerge your head alongside his body. Make sure he is holding his breath or blowing out. Check for bicycling and correct it by using the method described at left.

Combine Skills—By now your infant has learned to grasp the edge of the pool without your hand on his. He will automatically lift his head to get a breath on his own. Now it's time to teach him to do these things in combination with the kick-glide to the wall.

Don't wait until your baby has completely mastered the kick-glide. Include the grasping skill as soon as he can glide alone for several seconds at a time.

When you help your child learn to glide, release your supporting hands from his armpits a few feet before the wall. If he reaches out and grasps the side of the pool by himself, cuddle and praise him. If he does not, lift him out of the water by his hips and help him grasp the edge of the wall. Be sure he lifts his head to take a breath.

Repeat the exercise several times. As he nears the side of the pool, lift him by his hips and help him with his grasp. Do this every day until he grasps the side of the pool *by himself,* without coaching.

When your child can sit-dive, kick-glide to the wall and grasp the edge to breathe, he is *somewhat* safe in the swimming pool. But he is not yet *watersafe.*

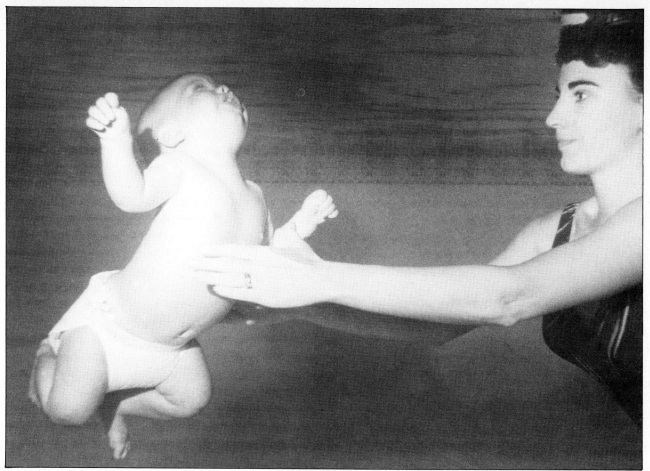

Submerge to check the progress of your baby as he attempts to kick-glide to the wall. Give him assistance if he needs it.

FREE BACK-FLOAT

By now your baby can comfortably float on his back with the light support of your hands on his head and buttocks. Go *slowly* with this next skill or your baby may become angry and afraid. Take several days at least, and be patient.

Create Atmosphere of Trust—Begin by holding your baby in the *cradle position* on his back with your hands securely under his head and buttocks. Play with him and sing to him. These are teachable moments. You have your infant's complete attention, confidence and trust. He feels safe in your hands.

Do nothing to shatter your infant's confidence. Slowly, almost imperceptibly, ease his body into the water until his ears are covered. Keep him in this position until he feels comfortable. Sing and talk gently to him all the time.

Gradually Remove Support—Slowly move your hand from under your infant's buttocks until it rests on his upper back. Ease your other hand

Place your hands under his head and buttocks to give him support.

Let her head rest on your wrists and lower arms.

down so both hands support his shoulder blades. Let his head rest on your wrists and lower arms.

Almost imperceptibly move your hands up until they support only the back of your baby's head. The rest of his body is floating freely in the water. It may take a long time and a lot of patience to accomplish this skill.

If your baby is tense or resists too much, *stop* the exercise. Restore support to his head and buttocks. Bounce him in the water and comfort him until he is relaxed and reassured.

Stroke Him into Floating—Your hands are now resting gently under the back of your baby's head. It is time to begin to stroke his head gently with alternating hands, slowly pulling one hand out from under his head and replacing it immediately with the other. You are alternately releasing the support of each hand in a soothing, continual stroking motion.

After your baby gets used to having his head stroked in the back-float position, gradually increase the amount of time you take between your hand strokes. Allow several seconds to pass with no support under your baby's head.

Gradually permit the lapse between direct support and free floating to increase. Soon your baby can float several minutes with only short assists. When he no longer needs assistance and can float by himself, he has mastered the free back-float.

Be Friendly—Keep your face directly above your child's so he can see your eyes. This gives him a feeling of security and companionship. If the sun is in his eyes, shield him with the shadow of your body. Sing and talk to him in soothing tones.

When you release your support from your baby's head, he may start to sink and get water in his nose. A wave may wash over his face even when you are supporting him with your hand. Restore your support before his nose sinks, and avoid waves as much as possible. Surprise submersions often result in gagging from sucked-in water.

Flexible Lesson Length—Be flexible about the length of the lesson when you teach your child the free back-float. If he seems happy and relaxed on his back, don't get out of the pool just because your 30 minutes are up.

Be patient. If your child is relaxed with the back-float, he might even fall asleep in the water!

ROTATING FROM STOMACH TO BACK

Next, your baby will learn the most important skill in the water-safety program. When he has

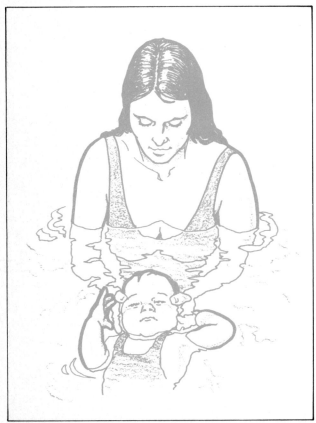

Slowly move your hands up so they support the back of her head.

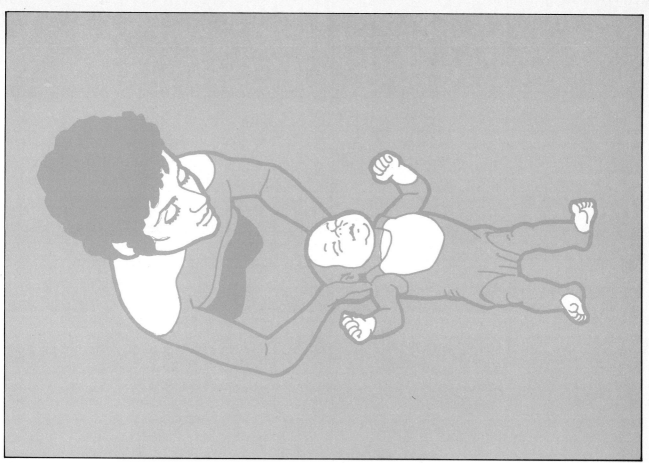

Gently stroke her head with alternating hands when she is relaxed in the water.

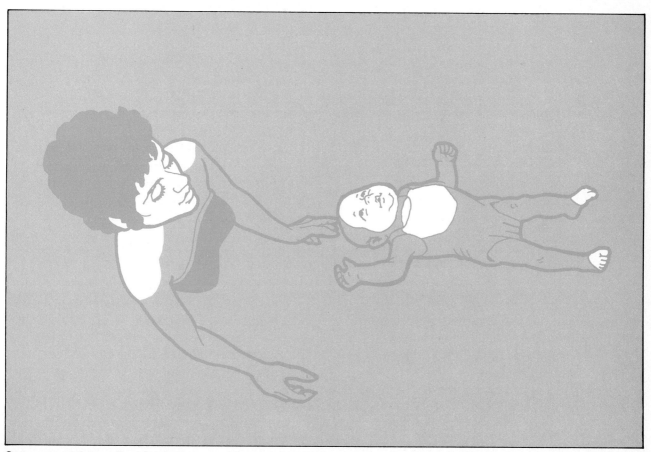

Soon your child can float freely by herself several minutes with only short assists from you.

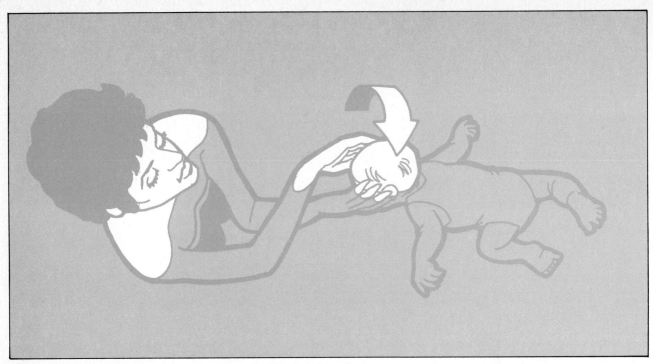

Cross your right wrist over your left wrist and hold baby's temples.

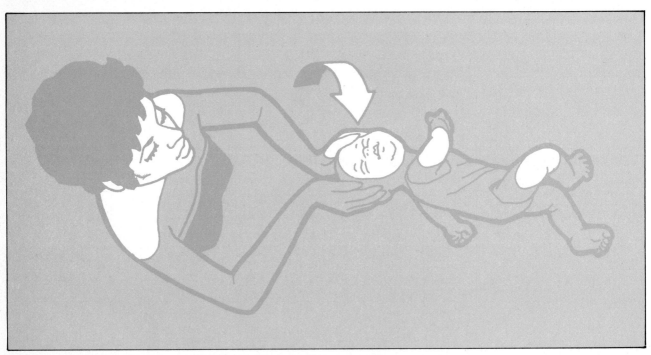

Turn your child on her back by rotating her clockwise with your hands.

mastered it, he can rotate from his stomach to his back so he can rest and breathe—all on his own!

Start with Sit-Dive—Place your baby on the edge of the pool in the sit-dive position. Glide him headfirst into the water.

Do not turn your back to the wall, as you are accustomed to doing in this exercise. Move about 5 feet away from the wall. Beckon your child toward you with your arms. You may submerge or not, according to your preference.

When your baby kicks to you, rise to the surface if you are submerged. Your baby is now directly in front of you on his stomach in the horizontal swim position.

Reach out and cross your right wrist over your left wrist in front of you. Place your right hand on his right temple and your left hand on his left temple. Turn him on his back by rotating his head clockwise with your hands. Smile at your baby when his face turns up out of the water.

Wait and see if he turns over on his back by himself. If he doesn't, turn him from his front to his back.

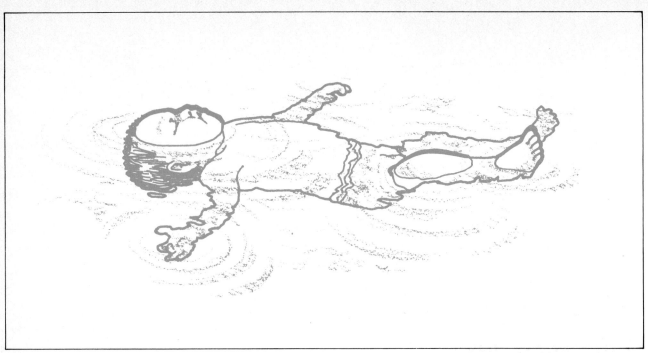

If your watersafe child should fall in the water, rescuers will probably find him floating on his back.

If your baby does not immediately begin to float on his back by himself, take the following steps. Begin stroking the back of his head as you did when teaching him the free back-float. Gradually increase the time lapse between strokes until he floats on his own.

When you feel your baby is performing this skill well, try some variations. Have your baby swim toward you, then gently turn him over on his back for air. Also, have him release his hold on the pool wall and float on his back.

Practice these exercises. Repeated drills help your baby learn faster. It may take several lessons to master this skill.

Add Variety—Do this exercise under many circumstances. You want your baby to turn onto his back automatically without thinking, no matter what his situation is in the water.

Try the rotation without the sit-dive from the side. Release your baby on his stomach, back away 5 feet and beckon him to kick to you. Place crossed hands on his temples and rotate him clockwise on his back. Try this in several areas of the shallow end of the pool.

Have your child kick to you when you are standing with your back to the wall. Let him grasp the edge and lift his head for a breath. Pull his hand from the pool wall, so he's back on his stomach in the horizontal swim position. Place crossed hands on his temples and rotate him onto his back.

Practice—Take your time with this important skill. You are teaching your child a new habit. Habits take time to acquire.

Rotate your baby with your hands for several lessons before you let him try to turn over on his own. If he needs more time to learn this skill, give it to him.

When you feel your baby is ready, release him, back away and beckon to him. When he reaches you, do not put out your hands to touch his temples. Wait and see if he turns over on his back by himself. If he does not, help him.

When your baby finally turns over on his back by himself, reward him with your approval. Have him practice this skill in several areas of the shallow end of the pool, under many circumstances.

HE IS WATERSAFE!

Your baby is now as watersafe as any infant can be. If he accidentally falls in some water, he won't sink or panic. Rescuers will probably find him floating on his back, patiently waiting for help.

What's Next—After your baby has completed this course, keep up his water-safety training. Go in the pool at least once a week to review the skills he has learned. Even though he is watersafe, never leave him alone in or around any water.

When your child is older, he can progress to the more-advanced Toddler training, beginning on page 65. Read that section and begin at the skill level your child has reached. When he is ready for swimming skills, teach him yourself with a good self-help manual.

Infant's Achievement Scorecard

Cuddling and praising your infant are wonderful rewards.

Use this scorecard to chart your baby's progress. Record his age as each new skill is mastered.

___ Fear is overcome. Your infant enjoys the water.

___ Submerges in the upright position with your help. Holds his breath or blows out underwater.

___ Glides to the wall on his stomach with your assistance.

___ Glides to the wall on his stomach without your assistance. Grasps the wall and holds onto side of pool.

___ Grasps the wall, holds on and lifts his head for breath.

___ Back-floats with your support. Floats on his back for a few seconds at a time.

___ Back-floats for several minutes without your support.

___ Back-floats without your support.

___ Sit-dives from the side. Turns around and kick-glides back to you at the wall. Grasps the wall, holds on and lifts his head for a breath.

___ Rotates from stomach to back to catch a breath. Floats.

___ Sit-dives from the wall and kick-glides several feet. Turns on back to catch breath. Remains floating on his back.

___ Sit-dives from the wall and kick-glides several feet. Turns on his back to catch breath. Turns back on his stomach and kick-glides back to the wall. Grasps the edge, holds on and lifts his head for a breath. Returns to back-float position.

Toddler Program

Your toddler's progress in learning water safety and survival depends on many things. Temperament, age and muscle coordination influence his speed of learning. Your ability to teach and effectively communicate with your child are also important. If your infant completed the Infant program, review the basics and begin at the skill level your child has reached.

We divided this course into eight week-long segments to organize lessons. It's not a rigid schedule to follow without change. The weekly plan for building skills is only a *general* guideline.

Some techniques are harder to learn than others and require more time and practice. Let your child master each skill at his own pace. Never compare his progress to other children's.

We describe each skill separately. When you teach, present them in various combinations. At each lesson review old skills and introduce new ones. Your child will put all the skills together to be watersafe.

During every lesson, praise your toddler. Hug him and pat him on the back. Let him know you are proud of what he is accomplishing.

Encourage him to think *I can* and *I will.* If he believes he can master a skill, he will. Give him time.

Sing and play games. Enjoy your time together in the pool. Never forget this rule: play and work are important parts of the program.

Week One

Spend the first lessons making your toddler comfortable in the water. Enter the pool gradually. Invent games and songs. When you introduce the first water-safety skill, treat it like another game.

BLOWING BUBBLES

Hold your child at on his tummy in the *horizontal swim position.* Place a pingpong ball on the surface of the water, directly in front of your face. Submerge your mouth and chin so they are just below the surface. Blow on the pingpong ball with strong puffs of air from your loosely closed mouth. Your child will be delighted as he watches the ball scoot across the water.

Next, let him blow the ball across the water by

Teach your toddler to blow bubbles by using a pingpong ball.

himself. Make sure he submerges so his chin and lips are below the surface of the water. Tell your child to blow on the ball with air from his mouth, not his nose. Be sure your toddler keeps his mouth almost closed as he blows. He may be so interested in this game he'll forget his lips are in the water.

As the game progresses, use the word "bubbles" frequently. Say, "Blow bubbles, James! Look how James can blow bubbles."

FLUTTER-KICK WITH KICKBOARD

The kickboard is for toddlers 16 months or older. If your child is younger than this, his legs are not strong enough to move the board through the water.

Teach Kicking First—Before you try the kickboard, show your child how to do the flutter-kick. This kick begins at the hip rather than the knee.

Show your toddler the correct way to kick by doing it yourself. Hold the side of a kickboard to demonstrate. Kick your legs in a regular rhythm from your hips. Keep your knees relaxed but straight, and splash your feet out of the water a little.

Ask your child to copy you. Say, "Now it's your turn, Billy. Let's see your splashes on top of the water."

Tell your toddler to face you and put his arms around your neck. Grasp his legs at the knee. Move his legs up and down in an exaggerated manner.

Pick up his legs one at a time to show him how to kick with a straight knee. Splash his feet out of the water.

In the same position, let your toddler kick on his own. Use your hands to correct too much bending at the knee. Say the word "splash" often, so he will start kicking when he hears it.

Don't worry about perfecting your toddler's kick at this time. Give him the general idea so he can effectively use the kickboard.

Move your child's legs up and down so they splash out of the water.

Introduce Kickboard—Your goal is to teach your toddler to push his kickboard through the water with the power of his legs. The board provides a resting place for his arms while he concentrates on his kick. He learns to float alone and overcome his urge to cling to you.

Treat the kickboard like a new toy. Tell your child to pretend it's a motorboat. Sing the songs suggested on page 43, or make up songs.

Provide Help—The kickboard may be awkward for your toddler. Until he is familiar with the board, don't expect him to use it alone.

Stand beside your child. Place him on his stomach so his torso is on the board and his legs extend over the end into the water. Tell him to clasp his hands on each side of the board. If he doesn't do this by himself, put your hands on top of his and hold them in place.

Stand directly in front of the kickboard so you face your child. Grasp the board with one hand and gently tow it along. Smile and sing the motorboat song.

Your child's torso should be on the kickboard, with legs extending into the water.

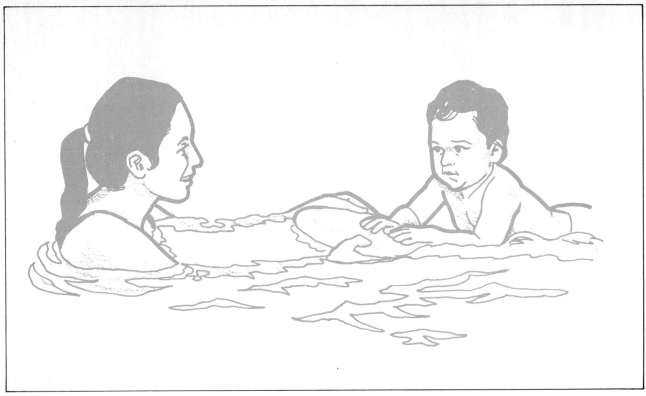

Stand in front of the kickboard, and tow it along.

After the first day, briefly let go of the board. Pull the board in front of you and let it go for a second or two. Grip the board again, stabilizing it, and tow it farther. Gradually let go of the board more often and for longer periods of time.

Encourage Him to Kick—When your child has a sense of balance on the kickboard, tell him to start kicking his legs. He will discover he can move the kickboard through the water on his own. Gradually lengthen the distance he covers on the board. If he shows no fear of the deep end, let him kick the length of the pool while you swim next to him.

SUBMERSION

The game with the pingpong ball teaches your child to exhale from his mouth while he's underwater. Now he is ready to submerge his face—nose and all.

Demonstrate for Him—Condition your child to exhale when he hears the word "bubbles." Say the word often when you are showing him how to submerge. Before you go under say, "Bubbles, Tommy. Watch Mommy blow bubbles!" Blow bubbles from your nose, so your child can see them rise to the surface.

You can also demonstrate with a waterproof doll that drinks and wets. Submerge the doll in an upright position. Squeeze its stomach so it blows

bubbles. Say, "Tommy, see your doll blowing bubbles?"

Join Him Underwater—Tell your child you're going underwater together. Tell him he can blow bubbles from his nose as well as his mouth. Tell him to keep his mouth almost closed and not to inhale.

Before you go under, smile and say, "Bubbles!" Grasp your youngster's shoulders with your hands and gently submerge him.

While underwater, make sure your child closes his mouth and blows bubbles from his nose. Notice if his eyes are open or closed.

Don't stay under for more than 5 seconds. Move your hands from your child's shoulders to his armpits, and pull him up out of the water.

As soon as you both break the surface, place your toddler's arms around your neck. Use your hands to move his legs in an extended flutter-kick. This distracts him from complaining about the submersion. It also reinforces his basic kicking instinct. As you move his legs, tell him how proud of him you are.

Common Problems—If your toddler gags from swallowed water, tell him to blow out from his mouth and nose to clear his throat. Don't go under again until he regains control of his breathing.

Your toddler may show a fear of submersion.

Go underwater with your toddler to teach him how to exhale.

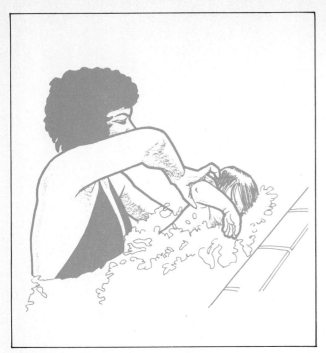

Move his arms up and down as you guide him to the wall.

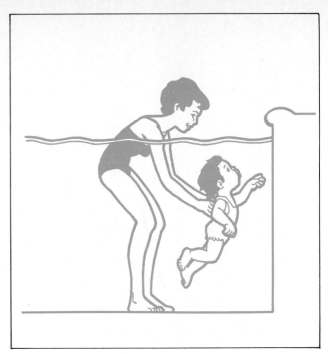

Submerge her as she reaches the wall.

This may be due to apprehension about being left alone in the water. Keep a loving hold on him at all times during your first submersions. Reassure him it's an enjoyable game you are playing together.

Your toddler may want to hold his nose with his thumb and finger. If he does this, invent underwater games that require him to use both hands.

Games help with the problems of closed eyes, too. Ask your toddler to count the number of fingers you are holding up underwater. When you surface, praise him when he tells you the correct answer.

GRASPING THE WALL

The ultimate goal of this water-safety program is to teach your toddler to propel himself to the wall, grasp it for support and lift his head to breathe. Start teaching him the grasping technique during the first few days of training.

Arm-Stroke—Tell your toddler you are going to help him "swim" to the wall. When he gets there, you want him to grasp the edge and lift his head out of the water.

Stand 3 feet from the pool wall, and place your toddler on your left side. Support the lower half of his body with your hip. Grasp the top sides of his arms, just above or below the elbows. Move his arms in and out of the water while you tow him to the wall. Keep a firm grip on his arms at all times. If he seems ready, encourage him to kick.

Help Him Grasp—When you reach the wall,

release the hold on your toddler's arms as his hands reach up to grip the wall. If necessary, direct his hands to the edge of the pool and wrap them over the edge. Tell him this is a good way to get his breath when he is playing in the water. Repeat the exercise twice.

Submerge His Head—Hold your child and paddle his arms toward the pool edge. This time submerge him as he reaches the wall. Release him as his hands reach up to grasp the edge of the pool. Explain that grasping the edge is a good way to get his face out of the water.

Praise your child! Don't let him complain about being submerged. Immediately distract his attention by putting him on the kickboard to play.

KICK-GLIDE TO THE WALL

By arm-stroking your child to the wall with your hands, you have prepared him for the next step in his training.

On His Own—Stand in the water about 5 feet from the wall, with your child on your left side. Face the wall. With your hands under his armpits, gently release him in a horizontal swim position. Allow him to submerge, kick-glide to the wall, lift his head for a breath and hold the edge. If he needs help, slowly and gently give him a push on the buttocks. He may or may not paddle with his arms as he kick-glides.

Repeat this exercise several times. Each time he grasps the wall, praise him. If necessary, distract him with the kickboard.

Don't Rush—You may feel nervous about letting

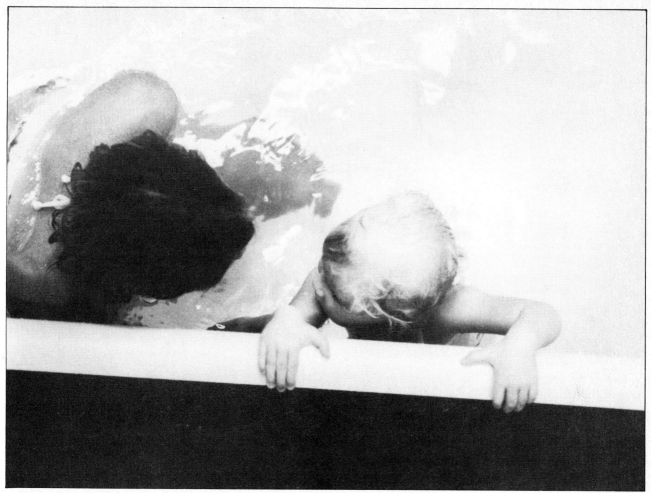

Your toddler should be able to grasp the edge of the pool without your assistance.

go of your toddler. Relax and do it. Your child will never learn if you don't let him go.

Don't rush this step in the lessons. If your child shows fear, you may have to hold his armpits all the way to the wall. When he shows more confidence, gradually release your support. He can do it—give him time.

Week Two

Your toddler is accustomed to the water by now although he may not be happy about submerging. Don't worry. His attitude will improve as he gains confidence. Review all the skills you have introduced before teaching new ones.

SIT-DIVE

This exercise is designed to accustom your toddler to the sensation of falling in the water. He will learn not to panic if he accidently falls in a pool.

Allow him to submerge and kick-glide to the wall.

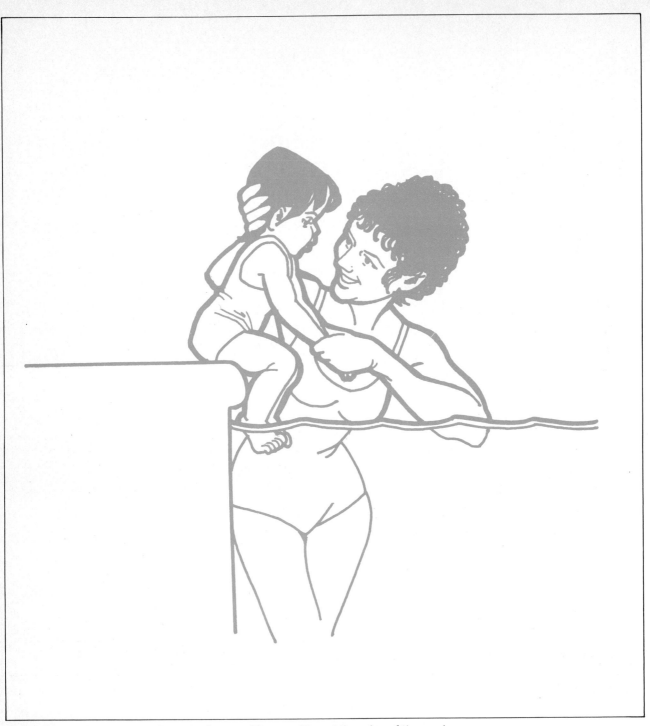

Guide your child down into the water from a sitting position at the edge of the pool.

Get Him Ready—Have your toddler kick-glide to the wall several times before you begin teaching the sit-dive. This reacquaints him with the horizontal swim position and the feeling of being on his own in the water.

When you feel he is ready, explain the next exercise to him. Tell him he is going to splash down from the side into the water. You will pull him a short distance from the wall. You expect him to return to the wall on his own, grasp it and pull his head up for air.

Use Your Hands—Help your child sit on the edge of the pool. Stand on his side, facing him with your hip touching the side of the pool. Hold both of his hands in your left one. Put your right hand behind his head.

Pull your toddler directly down in the water so his arms and head enter first. Let him glide out about 3 feet. He is underwater on his tummy in the horizontal swim position. You are still standing at the wall.

While he is underwater, grasp your toddler by

He is on his tummy in the horizontal swim position.

his waist and temple. Rapidly turn him around so he faces the wall. Allow your child to kick-glide back to the wall, grasp it and lift his head for a breath. Help him with a push on his buttocks, if necessary.

Praise your child when he performs the exercise. It's a big step for him, and he deserves applause. Immediately put him on the kickboard so he can rest and play.

Repeat the sit-dive several times each lesson. Give him any help he needs. Soon your toddler will be able to do it on his own.

Knee-Dive Variation—Have your toddler kneel on the edge of the pool with his legs folded under him. Pull him in the water, tow him and turn him around. Allow him to kick-glide back to the wall, grasp it and lift his head for a breath.

Sit-Slide Variation—If your child can't kick-glide to the wall, try this variation. Stand directly in front of your sitting toddler with your hands on his shoulders. Pull him head-first into the water. While he is submerged, let go of him with one hand. Quickly turn him around with your other hand, so he faces the wall.

Release his shoulder. He will kick his way up to the surface, grasp the pool edge and take a breath.

Grasp your toddler by his waist and temple.

In the sit-slide variation, turn her toward the wall.

Manually move your child's arms through the water.

ARM-STROKE

Your child is familiar with the arm-stroke. You have been moving his arms up and down with your hands while teaching him to grasp the edge of the pool.

Now your toddler must learn to move his arms and legs in the water. This helps him propel himself more quickly to the wall.

Guide your child through the arm-stroke exercises below.

Step 1—Place your toddler at your side or over your knee in the horizontal swim position. Grasp the top sides of his forearms below the elbows. Sing the "Row, row, row your boat" song as you manually move his arms up and down through the water. See page 43.

You are teaching him an exaggeration of the stroke he will use. You exaggerate the stroke at this stage so he learns the up-and-down movement he will need for stroking.

Continue this exaggerated up-and-down stroke as you submerge your child's face and tow him to the wall. Repeat. Then let him try moving his arms and legs as he kicks to the wall by himself.

Step 2—Tell your toddler you want him to imitate

the movements of your arms as he kicks to you. Stand in front of him. As he begins kicking through the water in the horizontal swim position, back away so he follows you across the pool.

Move your arms in front of his face in a rapid paddling motion. Make your movements below his eye level, so he can see them as he looks down in the water.

After 5 seconds, lift your child up for a breath. Again tell him to imitate your arm movements. Submerge him and back away as before, demonstrating the paddling motion in front of his face. Continue this until you cross the pool together.

When your child masters the paddling motion, stand 5 feet from the wall with him. Let him kick-paddle to the wall by himself. Praise him as he grasps the edge and comes up for a breath.

KICKING

By now your child enjoys the kickboard. He is learning to kick-paddle to the wall on his own. Now it's time for him to perfect his flutter-kick skills.

Check for Problems—Watch your child kick. Are his knees straight? Is he using both legs? Does he have good speed and rhythm?

If you notice any problems with your toddler's kicking techniques, stop and demonstrate on the kickboard how to do it correctly. Kick your legs in a regular rhythm from your hips. Keep your knees relaxed but straight. Kick your feet so your child can see the correct way to do it.

Make It Fun—Do playful things with your toddler's legs. Move them from side to side, then up and down. Tickle his toes. Help your child learn rhythm by singing songs like "Loup-T-Lou" on page 43. Sing while you practice the flutter-kick together. Hold the edge of the pool and kick your legs in the water. See who can make bigger splashes.

Fun with a Hoop—Your child will love this exercise. Tie a plastic hoop to a rock to keep it upright in the water. Place the hoop about 5 to 8 feet from the wall.

Stand 3 feet from the hoop, holding your child at your side. Release him and let him kick and arm-paddle through the hoop, propel himself to the wall and grasp it.

Watch for any problems in your toddler's kicking skills. Correct them by physically guiding his legs with your hands.

Trick Him into Kicking—What if your child will not kick by himself? What if he simply lies face-

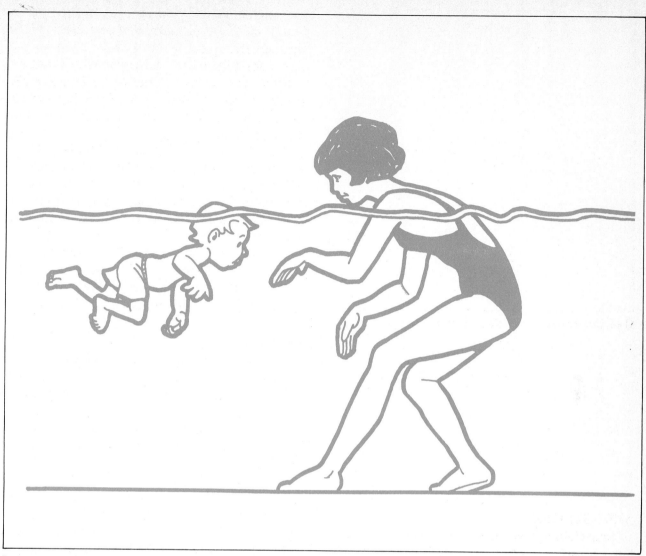

Paddle your arms underwater in front of your toddler's face.

down in the water and refuses to move his legs.

Try this trick. Stand 3 feet from the wall and hold your child at your side in the horizontal swim position. Push him off by his buttocks so he glides to the wall. Before he grabs the wall, take a firm grip on his left arm just below the shoulder. Use enough pressure to keep him submerged so he can't come up for a breath.

In his frustration, your toddler will begin to kick. As soon as he does, release him and allow him to grasp the wall. Praise him for his kicking ability. Repeat the exercise until he kicks to the wall on his own.

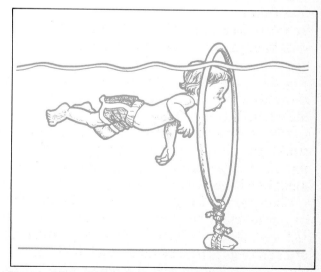

Your toddler will enjoy kicking through a hoop.

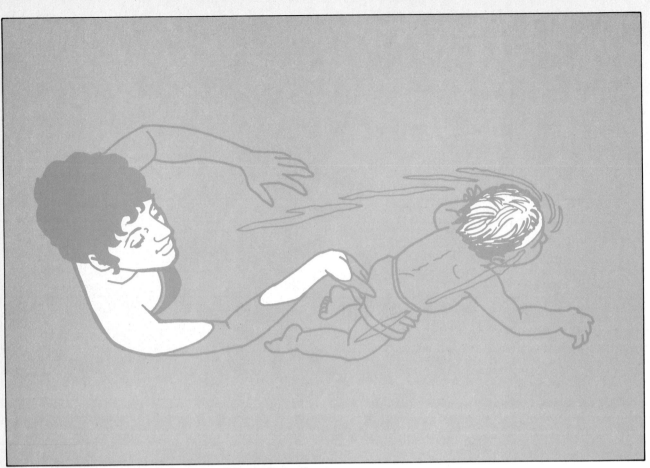

Give him a boost on the buttocks so he glides to the wall.

Keep your toddler submerged by grasping his arm for a few seconds. He'll kick to get to the surface.

Week Three

By now your child feels secure in the water. Success at learning makes him trust you as a teacher. He is willing to tackle more difficult challenges.

BACK-FLOAT

The back-float is an insecure position for your toddler because he feels unsupported. This triggers his instinctive fear of falling. Cuddle and play with him before you begin this lesson.

Ease Him into It—Stand in shoulder-deep water. Hold your toddler with his back toward you. Tell him to rest his head on your shoulder. The lower part of his body is extended in the water.

Your child's legs will rise to the surface. Point out how easily his legs float on the water. Sing and play, and let him enjoy the sensation of floating.

Move to Horizontal Position—When your child is relaxed on your shoulder, *slowly* move him down, easing his torso, then head, into the water. When he's in the horizontal position, put one hand under his buttocks and the other under his head.

Allow your toddler to relax as you slowly walk around the pool, singing and talking in a soothing manner. Have him stretch out his arms so they are supported by the water. Tell him to keep his stomach up and his legs straight. This is the ideal back-float position.

Bouncing Exercise—If your toddler seems afraid and resists the back-float, hold him in the *cradle position* with your hands on his head and buttocks. Move through the water, first up and down, then in circles.

Gradually lower your child into the water as you bounce him a little deeper each time. If you are careful not to frighten him or submerge his face, he'll enjoy this exercise.

Gradually Remove Support—Slowly move your hand from under his buttocks until it rests on his upper back. Ease your other hand down so both hands support his shoulder blades. Let his head rest on your wrists and lower arms.

Almost imperceptibly move your hands up until they support only the back of your toddler's head. The rest of his body is floating freely in the water. It may take a lot of time and patience to accomplish this.

If your child tenses up or resists, stop the exercise. Don't let him arch his back or try to sit up.

Rest his head on your shoulder, with his lower body in the water.

Slowly walk around the pool, singing and talking in a soothing manner. Your child can hold a toy if she wants to.

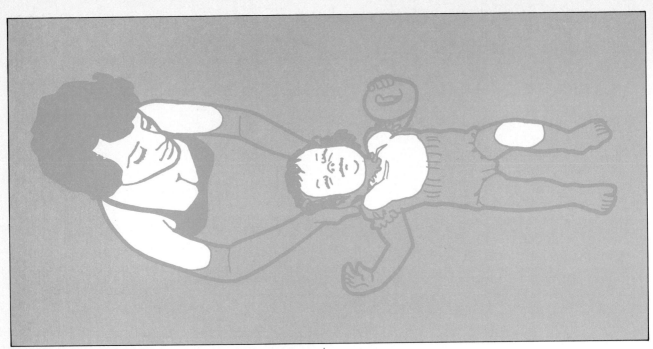

Slowly move your hands up so they only touch the back of the head.

After stroking the head, allow seconds to pass with no support.

Restore support to his head and buttocks, and bounce him playfully in the water. Sing to him and comfort him until he relaxes.

Stroke Him into Floating—Your hands now rest under the back of your toddler's head. Gently stroke his head with alternating hands. Slowly pull one hand out from under his head and immediately replace it with the other. You are alternately releasing the support of each hand in a soothing, continual stroking motion.

After your child gets used to having his head stroked in the back-float position, gradually increase the amount of time between hand strokes.

Allow several seconds to pass with no support under your toddler's head.

Permit the lapse between direct support and free-floating to increase. Soon your child can float several minutes with only short assists. When he no longer needs assistance, he has mastered the back-float.

Finger Hold—If your child doesn't object to the back-float position, use this method. Move your hands from your child's head and buttocks to his shoulder blades. Let his head rest on your wrists and lower arms. Move your hands up until they support only the back of his head.

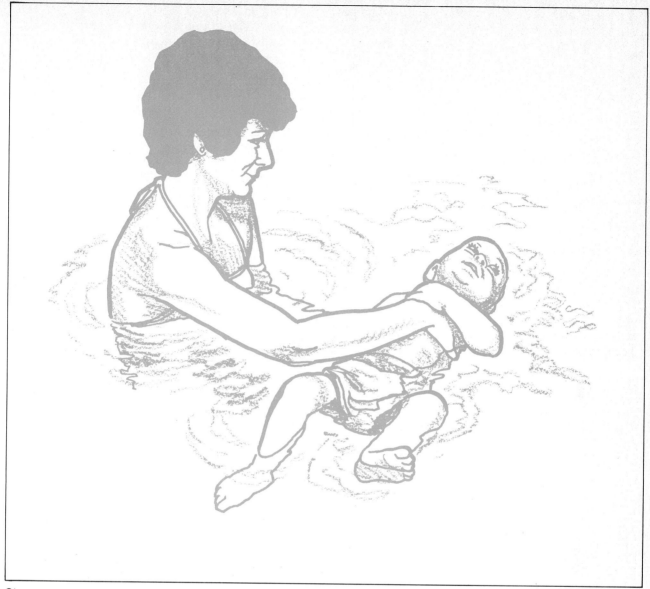

Sing the motorboat song as you move your child around in a circle.

When your child feels comfortable in this position, lighten your touch on his head until you support him with only two fingers of each hand. Gently release your fingers for brief periods, then restore support again.

Gradually increase the time your youngster floats on his own. Continue the exercise until he can float without assistance.

Leg Wrap—Here is another exercise to get your child accustomed to the back-float. Ask him to face you and wrap his legs around your waist. His head and torso are in the water, and your hands support him under his upper back. When he is used to this position, move your hands down under his hips.

Sing to him as you walk in circles around the pool. Bounce him lightly up and down on the surface of the water. When he feels at ease, remove his legs from your waist. Use the stroking or finger-hold technique to coax him into the back-float.

Motorboat—This is another back-float exercise. Stand at your toddler's side and place him on his back with your hands under his armpits. Move him in a circle as you sing the motorboat song found on page 43. Move him slowly at first, then pick up tempo as you sing faster. Reverse your direction and continue the same motion. Keep your hands under his armpits. Your toddler will love this exercise.

Make It Fun—Keep your face directly above your child's so he can see your eyes. This gives him a feeling of security. If the sun is in his eyes, shield him with the shadow of your body. Sing and talk to him in soothing tones.

When you release support from your toddler's

head, he may start to sink and get water in his nose. A wave may wash over his face even as you support him with your hand. Restore your support before his nose sinks. Avoid waves as much as possible. Surprise submersions often result in gagging from sucked-in water.

Flexible Lesson Length—Don't be rigid about the length of the lesson as you teach your child the back-float. If he seems to be happy and relaxed on his back, don't get out of the pool because 30 minutes are up. Be patient and flexible. If your toddler relaxes, he might even get sleepy in the water.

ROTATING FROM STOMACH TO BACK

Now your toddler will learn another important life-saving skill. When he masters it, he can rotate from his stomach to his back to rest and breathe.

Start with Sit-Dive—Tell your child you want him to dive from the side, then kick and paddle to you. Stand 5 feet from the pool wall and wait for him. When your toddler is in front of you on his stomach in the horizontal swim position, take the next step.

Cross your arms. Place your right hand on his right temple and your left hand on his left temple.

Guide him down to the toy with your hand on his arm.

Turn him on his back by rotating his head clockwise with your hands. Greet your toddler with a big smile when his face turns up out of the water.

Add Variety—Do this exercise under many circumstances. You want your child to turn on his back automatically, without thinking, no matter what his situation is in the water.

Try rotation without the sit-dive. Release your toddler on his stomach, back away 5 feet and beckon him to kick-paddle to you. Place crossed hands on his temples and rotate him clockwise on his back. Try this in several different areas of the shallow end of the pool.

Have your child kick and paddle to you while you are standing with your back to the wall. Let him grasp the edge and lift his head for a breath. Pull his hand from the pool wall, so he's on his stomach in the horizontal swim position. Place crossed hands on his temples and rotate him to his back.

Practice—Take your time with this important skill. You are teaching your child a new habit. Habits take time to acquire.

Rotate your toddler with your hands for several lessons before you let him try to turn over on his own. If he seems to need more time to learn this skill, give it to him.

When you feel your child is ready, release him, back away and beckon. When he reaches you, don't touch his temples. Wait a few seconds to see if he turns on his back himself. If he doesn't, help him.

When your toddler turns on his back, reward him with your approval. Have him practice this skill in several areas of the shallow end of the pool, under many circumstances.

Week Four

Review the skills your child has learned. Put special emphasis on the back-float and turning from his stomach to his back.

DIVING FOR TOYS

For this exercise you will need a submergible rubber toy. Or tie a fishing sinker to one of your child's favorite waterproof toys.

Hand It to Him—Tell your child to sit-dive or knee-dive into the water from the edge of the pool near the steps. Or let him stand on the steps and guide him into a dive with your hands on his head. Hold the toy underwater, and hand it to him while he is submerged. Gradually hold the toy deeper and deeper.

Release your child on her stomach, rotate her as soon as she kicks to you, and watch as she propels herself back to the wall.

Play "Fetch"—Throw the toy in the water and let it sink to the bottom. Ask your toddler to dive for it. If necessary, guide him down to the toy with your hand on his arm just below the shoulder. If he misses the toy as he searches the bottom, pick it up and hand it to him.

Use downward pressure to glide him into the water.

Have someone waiting to help your child up from the bottom.

Release your child's arm and let him kick to the surface. Put your hand under his armpit to pull him up for a breath. Push his buttocks so he kicks and paddles to the wall. Repeat this exercise until he kicks to the bottom, retrieves the toy and comes up without assistance.

For variation, have your child rotate from his stomach and float on his back instead of moving to the wall. Praise him and show your delight when he hands you the toy.

Move to Deeper Water—Use the toy to acquaint your toddler with the deep end of the pool. Hold the side or tread water while you throw the toy and wait for it to sink.

Tell your child to knee-dive off the side and kick his way down to retrieve the toy. You'll be delighted by his ability to do this in deep water.

DIVING

Once your child can dive, he won't be surprised by an accidental fall in the water.

Off the Edge—Tell your toddler to stand on the edge of the pool at the shallow end. Stand in the water in front of him.

Place one of your hands under your child's stomach and the other behind his head. Use downward pressure to glide him into the water. Release him and allow him to kick to the surface. Boost him on the buttocks to guide him to the wall.

Off the Board—Walk your child to the end of the diving board. When he is standing on the edge, have him jump off so he enters the water feet first.

Have someone waiting in the water to help your child up from the bottom. Let your toddler jump off the board several times before you teach him to dive.

Diving on His Own—Your toddler should stand on the side of the pool. Have him lean over and touch his toes. His face is down, looking at the water.

Standing next to him, place your right hand on his buttocks and your left hand on the back of his head. Use enough pressure to keep his face looking down.

Guide your child into the water by giving him a slight push forward and down. Have someone waiting in the water to help him up from the bottom. If necessary, this person guides your toddler to the side of the pool after he surfaces.

Use the same technique to teach your youngster to dive off the board. Have an assistant help him up from the bottom.

Before she dives off the side, be sure your child is looking down.

On the count of 4, lift your child by the T-shirt so he can get a breath.

Firmly pull up to lift his face out of the water.

Weeks Five to Nine

The next four weeks of teaching are presented in one section. You will concentrate on teaching one new skill— *breathing*.

FACE-LIFT BREATHING

This skill takes several weeks to learn. Don't rush your toddler. Fill the lesson with play and review skills he already knows.

Use a T-Shirt—Put a T-shirt over your toddler's swimsuit. Stand in the water about 10 feet from the wall. Hold him at your left side in the horizontal swim position.

Use your right hand to grasp the T-shirt between your child's shoulder blades. Move with him as he kick-paddles toward the wall. Have him keep his face in the water. Make sure he blows bubbles by exhaling through his nose and mouth.

Count to Four—As you walk beside your toddler, loudly and slowly count to three. When you get to four, stop! Firmly pull up on your child's T-shirt to lift his face out of the water. Allow him to get a breath of air—make sure he takes it.

After your child inhales, lower his body so his face is in the water. Release his T-shirt and allow him to kick and paddle to the wall and grasp the edge.

As you repeat this exercise, gradually decrease the amount of help you give your toddler. Instead of firmly lifting him up with your hand, make your pull gentle and light. Let him do most of the lifting by himself.

Lower Your Hand—Instead of grasping the T-shirt by the shoulders, hold the bottom of the shirt. Use the same hand to grip your child's swimsuit above the buttocks. Your support is at the bottom of your toddler's back.

Move your child to the wall on a four-count. Stop on count four until he lifts his head for a breath. Provide only gentle assistance.

If He Won't Come Up—Move with your toddler to the wall with your hand on his T-shirt. Slowly count to three. Stop on four and hold your child in place. Don't allow him to go forward until he lifts his head for a breath.

Repeat this exercise until your toddler comes up on the count of four. You are still providing help with your hand, but your touch is light and minimal.

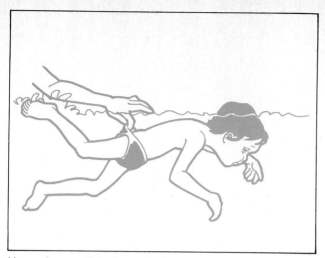

Use only your thumb and forefinger.

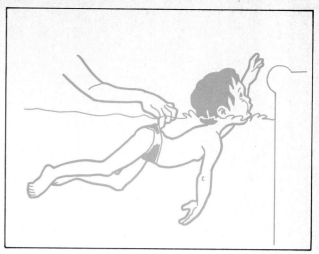

Next, use only your forefinger.

Without T-Shirt—Grip your toddler's swimsuit at his buttocks. Move him to the wall for three counts. Stop on four until he lifts his head for a breath. Release your grip and let him kick and paddle to the wall.

Loosen your grip on his swimsuit so you hold it by your thumb and forefinger. Next, use only your forefinger for support.

Your child senses your loosening hold on him, but his confidence in himself is growing. Praise him when he lifts his head on his own.

By Himself—Walk behind your toddler as he kick-glides to the wall. Your forefinger is hooked into his swimsuit above the buttocks. Count to three. As your child begins to lift his head for air on count four, let go of his suit. Make him come up for air by himself.

At first your toddler may be angry because you didn't help him when he expected it. For this reason, do this exercise only a few times each lesson.

Bicycling—As your toddler learns to come up for air by himself, he may move into a vertical position and tread water. This is called *bicycling*. Your child gets nowhere while he is bicycling. He can't kick and paddle to the wall. He flounders and becomes exhausted.

Correct bicycling by submerging yourself on your back a few feet below your child's body. Move slowly backward below him as he moves to the wall. Your toddler will move into the correct horizontal position as he looks down at your face.

When your child has kicked and paddled 5 to 8 feet, stand up. Lift him up for a breath by pulling on his swimsuit. Repeat this procedure many times. Soon your child realizes he goes faster and breathes more easily when he's in the horizontal position.

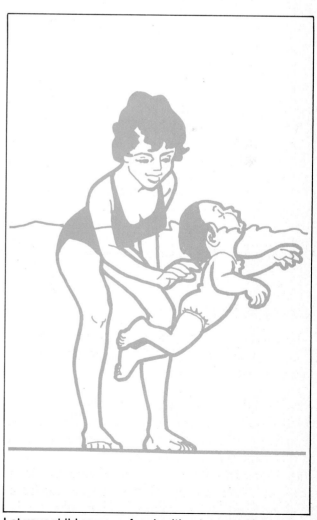

Let your child come up for air without your assistance.

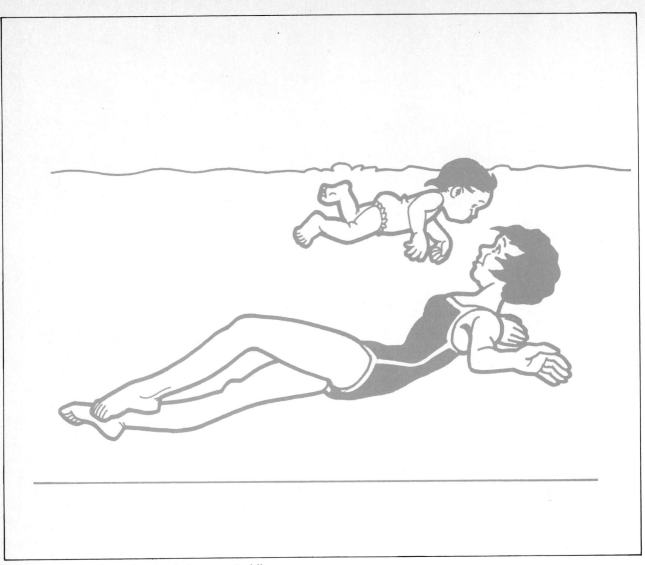
Correct bicycling by swimming below your toddler.

HE IS WATERSAFE!

Your toddler is now as watersafe as any child can be. If he accidentally falls into a body of water, he won't panic and sink. Rescuers will probably find him floating on his back, patiently waiting for help. Or he may be at the side of the pool, climbing out of the water on his own.

What's Next—When your toddler completes this course, continue water-safety training. Go in the pool at least once a week to review the things he's learned. Even though he is watersafe, never leave him alone in or around any water.

Soon you'll want your child to progress to swimming skills. Enroll him in a class or teach him yourself with a good self-help manual.

You'll be proud to see he's not a screaming, frightened, clutching beginner. In his early years, you have taught him to be confident in the water.

Even though your child is watersafe, watch him closely when he is near water.

Your child can lift her head to breathe on her own while she propels herself to safety.

Toddler's Achievement Scorecard

Use this scorecard to chart your child's progress. Record his age as each new skill is mastered.

___ Fear is overcome. Your child enjoys the water.

___ Blows bubbles underwater from his mouth and nose.

___ Balances on the kickboard.

___ Flutter-kicks on the kickboard.

___ Submerges in the upright position with your help. Exhales underwater.

___ Opens his eyes underwater.

___ Reaches up, grasps the wall, holds on and lifts his head for a breath.

___ Glides to the wall in a horizontal position with your assistance.

___ Kick-glides to the wall on his own from a distance of 5 feet. Reaches up, grasps wall, holds on and lifts his head for a breath.

___ Sit-dives from the side. Turns around and kick-glides back to the wall.

___ Knee-dives from the side. Turns around and kick-glides to the wall. Reaches up, grasps wall, holds on and lifts his head for a breath.

___ Combines the arm-paddle with kicking.

___ Perfects his flutter-kick.

___ Back-floats with your support. Free-floats on his back for seconds at a time.

___ Back-floats for several minutes without your support.

___ Back-floats without your support.

___ Rotates from stomach to back to catch a breath. Floats.

___ Dives for toys in shallow water. Comes up for air and turns over to float on his back.

___ Dives for toys in deep water. Comes up for air, kicks and paddles to the wall, reaches up to grasp the edge, holds on and lifts head for a breath.

___ Stand-dives off the edge of the pool.

___ Jumps off the diving board.

___ Stand-dives off the diving board.

___ Lifts his head to take a breath with your hand on his T-shirt.

___ Lifts his head to take a breath with your hand on his swimsuit.

___ Lifts his head to take breaths on his own in a regular rhythm.

Questions & Answers

Q. What do you mean by water safety and survival?

A. An infant or toddler learns to be confident in the water without losing respect for it. In case of an accident, he can save his own life. He does not necessarily learn to swim.

Q. But if he doesn't learn strokes, what does he learn?

A. He learns two combinations of skills:
1. To turn himself on his back for a breath and to back-float.
2. To propel himself in the direction of the wall of the pool, grasp the edge and lift his head for a breath.

Q. At what age should a child begin a course in water safety and survival?

A. Newborns may be best equipped to handle water because of their recent nine months of exposure to it. However, 3 months old is the best age to start. Your infant is learning to control his muscles.

Your child will learn to float on her back.

Children under 4 years old are the most drown-prone. Water-safety training benefits them.

Q. Why do you choose these ages for teaching water safety and survival?

A. Children under 4 are the most drown-prone, yet they are excluded from many swimming classes. We feel there is a critical need for training in water safety for this age group.

Q. Why is it necessary for parents to teach their children?

A. It's not necessary, but your child will do better with you as his instructor. This is because of the trust he has in you. He feels confident when you're in the pool with him at all times, comforting, praising and hugging him.

Q. Can parents teach their infants and toddlers better than a well-trained instructor can?

A. There are few well-trained instructors for infants and toddlers. Your child responds better to you than to a stranger.

Q. Can this course give parents a false sense of security and lead to a relaxation of vigilance?

A. Not if they note our frequent warnings that no child is drownproof. This book should make parents more aware of their responsibility never to leave a child unattended in or near water.

Q. What if I am terrified of water myself? Won't this frighten my child?

A. Yes. However, because you won't be in water more than shoulder deep, this could be an opportunity for you to overcome your fear. If your fear is so intense that you can't overcome it, your spouse or some other person should substitute for you.

Q. How often are lessons necessary?

A. Lessons should take place every day. If your schedule does not allow this, give the lessons at least two or three times a week. Keep them on a regular basis to take advantage of force of habit.

Q. How long does it take to complete this training?

A. Infants and toddlers vary in learning speed. Frequency of lessons and other factors influence time required for success. In general, 2 to 3 months of consistent training can make your child watersafe.

Q. Can all children learn water safety and survival?

A. All of them can learn at least some of it. This includes handicapped children. Be careful not to compare your child to others or push him too fast.

Q. I can't swim but I'm not afraid of water. Can I teach my child water safety and survival?

A. Yes. Just follow the rules in this book.

Q. Do some parents become frustrated when trying to teach their children water safety?

A. Some parents have difficulty teaching their children motor skills. But most parents welcome this challenge as an opportunity to become closer to their child.

Q. How can I help my child remember what he learns in this course?

A. Take him to the pool at least once a week— summer and winter. Review the techniques he has learned.

Q. Must I stay on a one-to-one basis when I'm teaching my child in the pool?

A. Unless you are learning new skills or reviewing other skills, your family and friends can join in the waterplay with you and your child.

Your family and friends can join in waterplay with your child after you finish your lessons.

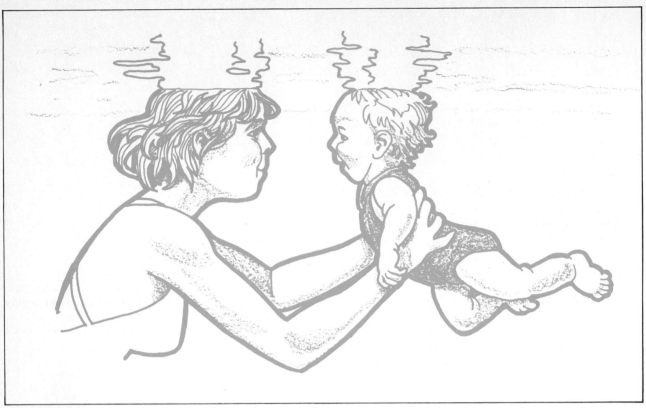

Your child shouldn't use waterwings or floating aids in the water. These devices give children a false sense of security.

Q. Are you opposed to inflatable floating aids such as waterwings?

A. We do not recommend these devices. They give your child a false sense of security. He may jump in the water without the device and expect the water to support him.

Q. You mention a child feels more secure in the upright position. Some systems allow children to remain in this position in the water. Why do you teach children to feel comfortable in the horizontal swim position?

A. Children flounder in the upright position. They bob up and down until they are exhausted. To swim successfully to the edge of the pool, a child must assume the horizontal swim position.

Q. We don't have access to a pool. Can we use our spa for teaching our child water safety?

A. Your spa is fine for teaching. Keep the water at a temperature of 90-92F (32-33C). Never use the bubbling air jets.

Q. What is the best temperature for the water in a swimming pool?

A. About 88F (31C) in the summer and 92F (33C) in the winter. If the water is too cold, it will shock your child. He can't learn when he is shivering. Keep the pool water about the same temperature as your child's bath water.

Q. I don't have a swimming pool and must go to a public pool. The water is not as warm as you recommend. What should I do?

A. Don't count on using the public pool. Health rules may not allow your infant or toddler to enter. Even if he can enter, the crowds will be distracting. Try to find a neighbor who has a pool. If she has an infant or toddler, they might want to learn water-safety techniques.

Q. Does swimming increase upper-respiratory infections in children?

A. According to the pediatricians who care for our students, the answer is no. But if a child has an infection, he should not have his lesson. Keep him out for awhile.

Q. Does water that gets in children's ears during swimming cause ear infections?

A. No. Infections begin in the throat and upper-respiratory organs, not in the outer ear. Always dry your child thoroughly after his lesson, especially in cooler weather.

Q. Besides a cold, what other illnesses can keep my child from taking a lesson?

A. Don't let your child go in the pool if he has a communicable disease like chicken pox, rubella or impetigo. If he seems tired, fretful or feverish, don't give him a lesson. When in doubt, consult your physician.

Q. How do I keep the water from becoming contaminated by urination or bowel movements?

A. You can't prevent some contamination. To make it minimal, dress your baby in tight-fitting disposable diapers covered by plastic pants. Take along extra diapers and change them immediately after soiling occurs. Pools that admit infants and toddlers who are not toilet trained must take extra precautions with maintenance.

Q. Can handicapped children be taught water safety and survival?

A. They may take more time to learn the skills, but mentally and physically handicapped children can complete the program. Check with your physician to see if you should take any special precautions when dealing with your child's handicap in the water.

Q. Are there occasions when a child becomes so unruly and uncooperative that he must be spanked?

A. Instead of spanking, try to understand why your child is refusing to cooperate. Is he afraid or tired? Have you taken the fun out of the experience? Are you overreacting to his behavior? The more upset you become, the more uncooperative he becomes. Take time out to play the next time you enter the water. However, do not reward his misbehavior with immediate playtime. The next time he'll know how to get out of working. Finish your activity, then play.

Q. You refer to a baby's exposure to water in the mother's uterus as a great plus for early training in water safety. Aren't you forgetting that a baby in the uterus doesn't have to worry about getting a breath of air?

A. No. That's why we stress your child shouldn't be kept underwater too long. Be sure he takes a good breath when he comes out of the water.

Q. What if my child hates water? Should I force him to learn water safety and survival?

A. Unless a child has had a bad experience, he will learn to love the water. Be slow and patient about introducing him to the pool. Let him start by sitting on the side and kicking his feet in the water. Later you can use games, praise, love and hugs to make him *want* to come into the water.

Q. Are some children so frightened of water that even this carefully supervised program is too traumatic for them?

A. This course is designed to help children over-

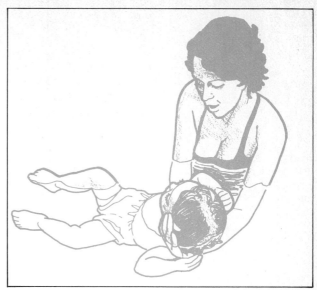

Handicapped children can also be taught water safety and survival.

Even though your child is watersafe, never let him go near the water by himself.

come their fear of water without losing their respect for it. A child's fear is the principal reason for having his parent as a teacher. Love is more powerful than fear. A child's parent is his best teacher—even if the child is frightened of the water.

Q. Is it necessary to repeat the course for a child to make him watersafe?

A. It takes some children longer to master skills. Instead of thinking in terms of repeating the course, spend enough time learning each new skill before you move on to the next one. After completing the course, go to the pool and review your child's skills at least once a week.

Index

A

Accidents 17, 19
Ages to begin 8
Alternatives to
  swimming pools 13
    bathtubs 13
    lakes 13
    oceans 13
    plastic wading pools 13
    spas 13
Arm floats 16
Arm-stroke 70, 74
Assisted back-float 51, 53
Assisted glide to the
  wall 47, 53

B

Baby's messages 29
Back-float position 51, 58, 77,
  78, 79
Bathing suit 15
Bathtub 14
Behavior modification 6
Behavior problems 41
Bicycling 56, 85
Blow on his face 45
Blowing bubbles 16, 18, 46,
  65, 68
Bouncing exercise 51, 77
Breath holding 47
Building skills 65
Burping 18

C

CPR 18
  for infants 20
  for toddlers 20-21
Choking 19
Clothes to bring 15
Communication 8, 26, 65
Cradle position 52, 57, 77

D

Daily lessons 14
Daily routine 14
Development
  intellectual 12
  physical 12
  social 12
Discouragement 10
Disposable diapers 15
Diving 82
Diving for toys 80
Drownings 6
Drownproof 6, 16

E

Ear infection 16, 19
Ear plugs 16
Example 39
Exhaling underwater 47
Eye contact 27

Eye messages 27

F

Face-lift breathing 84
Facial messages 27
Fears
  deep water 30
  falling 30, 52
  loud noises 30
  submersion 30
Firm expectations 37
Flotation devices 16
  arm floats 16
  waterwings 16
Food treats 36
Free back-float 57, 58, 62

G

Gagging 46
Games 65, 70
Getting ready 5
Glide 50, 51
Grasping reflex 50
Grasping the wall 50, 51, 70

H

Handicapped 39
Health 11
Holding the nose 70
Hoop 74
Horizontal back-float position
  51, 52
Horizontal swim position 47,
  50, 53, 60, 70, 72, 74, 75, 77

I

Illness 19
Infant fears 30
Infant games 35
Infant mental development 26
Infant motor development 26
Infant program 45-63
Infant skills 23
Infant's achievement
  scorecard 63
Infections 11

K

Kick-glide to the wall 55, 56,
  70, 72, 73
Kickboard 15, 35, 66, 73
Kicking instinct 68
Kicking problems 74
Knee-dive 80, 82
  variation 73

L

Learning patterns 26
Leg wrap 79
Lesson breaks 14

M

Material rewards 36
Mentally handicapped 39

Motivation 34
  rules 41
Motor skills 23
Motorboat 79
Muscle coordination 65
Music 28

N

Newborn babies 13
Nose plugs 16

O

Off the board 82
Older toddlers 25
One-to-one training 9
Overcoming fears 30

P

Parent-child relationship 7
Parents' fears 32
Patience 42
Physical guidance 39
Physically handicapped 39
Pingpong ball 16, 65, 68
Plastic wading pool 14
Play 8
Playing games 65
Position of the sun 14
Praise 65

Q

Questions and answers 91-95

R

Rewards 35
  approval 35
  as motivation 35
  example 35
  fun 35
Rotating from stomach to
  back 58, 80
Rules of motivation 41

S

Scorecard of achievement 6,
  63, 89·
Self-confidence 12
Sex 8
Sickness 19
Signs of fear 30
Signs of terror 32
  extreme limpness 32
  facial expression 31
  rigid arms and legs 32
  shivering uncontrollably 32
  what to do 32
Singing 28, 39, 65, 79
Sit-dive 53, 60, 71, 72, 80
Sit-slide variation 73
Snacks 15
Songs 43, 65
Sore throat 19
Special child 39

Special relationship 12
Spitting up 18
Storms 15
Stroke into floating 58
Stroking back of head 62
Submergible toys 16
Submersion 18, 45, 47, 53,
  68, 70
Sunglasses 27
Sunscreen 15
Survival float 6
Swallowing water 18, 55, 68
Swimming skills 62

T

Teachers 10
Temper tantrums 41
Temperament 65
Time of day for teaching 14
Toddler development 26
Toddler fears 32
Toddler games 35, 36
Toddler program 65-89
Toddler skills 23
Toddler's achievement
  scorecard 89
Toddlers 8
  older 8
  younger 8
Touch messages 28
Trinkets 36
Trouble signs 17
Types of pools 13
  indoor 13
  outdoor 13
  public 13

U

Underwater dangers 17
Underwater games 70

V

Voice messages 28
Vomiting 19

W

Water temperature 13
Waterplay songs 43
Waterproof doll 16
Watersafe 6
Waterwings 16
When to start 12

Y

Younger toddlers 24
Your child's development 23

4.628560 1137